FISHES OF THE ATLANTIC COAST

CANADA TO BRAZIL, INCLUDING
THE GULF OF MEXICO, FLORIDA, BERMUDA,
THE BAHAMAS, AND THE CARIBBEAN

408 FISHES IN FULL COLOR

BY

Illus

Graphic D

STANFORD UNIVERSITY PRESS
Stanford, California

This book is dedicated to Jacques Yves Cousteau,
fishwatcher and protector of the sea and all living things.
He says: "We still think of the sea as another world
populated by weird or fierce animals, when in fact there
is a striking unity of life above and under the surface of
the oceans, a similarity of motivation and behavior, and
an indefectible dependence of all forms of life, including
ours, upon the quality and vitality of our planet's
water system."

First edition published in 1976 as
*The Many-Splendored Fishes of the
Atlantic Coast including the Fishes of
the Gulf of Mexico, Florida, Bermuda,
The Bahamas and the Caribbean*,
by Marquest Colorguide Books;
reissued in 1985, with minor corrections,
by Stanford University Press; not
published in hardcover.

Stanford University Press
Stanford, California
© 1976 by Gar Goodson
Printed in Korea
ISBN 0-8047-1268-9
First printing of this edition 1976
Last figure below indicates year of this printing:
04   03   02

PREFACE

Although written primarily as a fishwatcher's guide, this book is also aimed at catching the interest of those who have never looked beneath the surface of the sea. West Atlantic reefs are a fishwatcher's paradise, as evidenced in these pages. There is no other experience in the world quite like a diver's first tour of an underwater reef. Whether in temperate waters or tropical coral reefs, one finds an unforgettable realm of oceanic blue, teeming reef fish colonies, towering, mysterious reef formations, brilliant sea grass and algae beds, all glistening and sparkling in the sea-filtered sunlight. No special diving skills, exotic equipment or deep water dives are required to make a tour of the reefs. Most of the fishes shown here can be seen while snorkeling on the surface over shallow water reefs (5 to 20 foot depths) with a face mask, snorkel tube and swim fins. The ability to swim is all that is required. See page 202 for diving tips for beginners.

This guidebook is designed for the fishwatcher; that non-technical, curious person, whether casual tourist-swimmer, skin or SCUBA diver, fisherman or aquarist who seeks to know more about the abundant and beautiful marine life of the West Atlantic. No special knowledge of fishes is required to comprehend this book other than a general understanding of fish anatomy. The illustration below identifies the chief parts of a typical fish.

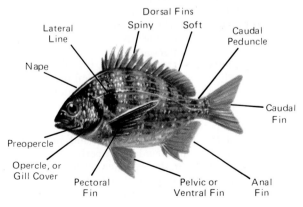

Dorsal Fins
Spiny   Soft

Lateral
Line

Caudal
Peduncle

Nape

Caudal
Fin

Preopercle

Opercle, or
Gill Cover

Pectoral
Fin

Pelvic or
Ventral Fin

Anal
Fin

I have sought to be as accurate as possible in describing in words and pictures 378 West Atlantic fish species, with particular focus on those commonly sighted by divers, taken by fishermen or collectors, or found in the marketplace. For each fish family I have provided information, when known, about behavioral and breeding patterns, color variations, attack and defense behavior and other distinguishing characteristics. For each fish species I have provided the common name in English, the Spanish common name (in parentheses), the scientific name, maximum size (total length), salient characteristics of the fish, range and edibility. One hundred and eighty-two of the 378 species described here, including virtually all of the common food and game fishes, have a Spanish common name. It is hoped that this will make the book helpful to Spanish-speaking, as well as English-speaking fish-watchers.

To assist the reader in visualizing the vast West Atlantic, and to aid in locating the range of specific fishes, I have provided maps of the area on pages 203 and 204. The West Atlantic is shown from Labrador to Brazil, along with a more detailed map of the Gulf of Mexico, Florida, the Bahamas and Caribbean areas. Of special interest to fishwatchers are the underwater parks. The John Pennekamp Coral Reef State Park in the Florida Keys (see page 204) is highly recommended for beginning divers and experienced aquanauts. The State of Florida has declared 75 square miles of splendid coral reef as an underwater park where no spear fishing or taking of reef animals is allowed. Buck Island near St. Croix in the U.S. Virgin Islands was declared a national monument by President Kennedy in 1961 because of the magnificent barrier reef surrounding the eastern half of the island. A remarkable underwater snorkeling trail has been provided for fishwatchers (see page 204). It is my hope that this book will encourage the establishment of many new underwater parks, trails and reefs throughout the West Atlantic.

A final and important objective of this book is to remind the coastal states of the U.S., and the islands of the West Indies, of the magnificent and highly perishable resource that lies just off their shores. New measures of conservation and reef management are critically needed. Most of our coral reefs are now still intact, but these fragile structures can be seriously damaged or destroyed by overfishing, careless coastal and harbor developments, landfills, sewage, industrial wastes and careless divers, fish collectors and fishermen. The recent butchering of Florida's coast by an army of bulldozers is a prime example of the danger threatening littoral zones throughout the West Atlantic.

The establishment of city, state and national underwater parks and preserves is a key step in reef preservation. Fishes and other creatures of the sea need not be hunted to extinction or driven from their habitats. They are fascinating, beautiful animals to study and admire, deserving of our care and concern. The wilderness question is especially applicable to the reefs of the West Atlantic. Will we have to tell our grandchildren about the wilderness that was, and the underwater world of the reefs that used to be? Or can we preserve these frontiers, so that they can find them as we did, and experience the same joy and admiration?

ACKNOWLEDGMENTS

I am especially indebted to Dr. Camm C. Swift, Associate Curator of Fishes at the Los Angeles County Museum of Natural History. His years of experience in the study of Florida and other West Atlantic fishes, his careful review of these pages prior to presstime, and his counseling and recommendations as to areas of research were invaluable aids in the preparation of this book. I am also indebted to Mssrs. J. E. Bohlke and C. G. Chaplin for their monumental work "Fishes of the Bahamas and Adjacent Tropical Waters," to Mr. J. E. Randall for his excellent "Caribbean Reef Fishes," to Mssrs. W. A. Starck and R. H. Chesher for their comprehensive work on Florida's Alligator Reef, to W. Beebe and J. Tee-van for their "Field Book of the Shore Fishes of Bermuda and the West Indies," and many others too numerous to mention here. Acknowledgements to these and many other authors whose works were valuable in compiling this book are made in a detailed bibliography and list of reference reading on page 191. Special appreciation is also due to Mr. R. Stuart Johnson, Vice President and Manager of the California First Bank in Manhattan Beach, California for his counseling in the considerable financing required to produce this book, and to Robert D. Kennedy for his willing assistance in the timetaking process of editing and review.

CONTENTS

FISHES OF THE ATLANTIC COAST

SEA BASSES AND GROUPERS

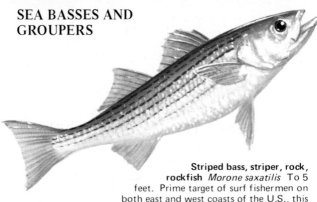

Striped bass, striper, rock, rockfish *Morone saxatilis* To 5 feet. Prime target of surf fishermen on both east and west coasts of the U.S., this splendid bass is sought for its tenacious fighting ability, its striped beauty and its excellence as a table fish. The rod and reel record is 72 pounds on 50 pound line. A temperate bass of the Percichthyidae family, the striped bass is anadromous like the salmon, migrating up streams to spawn. **Range:** St. Lawrence River to Florida and through the Gulf of Mexico to Louisiana. **Edibility:** excellent.

The West Atlantic is especially favored in having a splendid array of basses and groupers. They include some of the finest food fishes, and range in size from the tiny, brilliant basslets through the colorful hamlets to the large and magnificent striped, speckled and spotted groupers. The handsome striped bass excited the admiration of the early colonists to New England over 360 years ago. Captain John Smith wrote: "The basse is an excellent fish, both fresh and salte. They are so large, the head of one will give a good eater a dinner, & for daintinesse of diet they excell the Marybones of Beefe."

☐ Groupers and sea basses (family Serranidae) are bottom dwellers. They either sit on the bottom in caves or reef crevices or roam across the bottom. Many of them have large, gaping mouths indicating their carnivorous feeding habits. The identification and classification of the serranids has been and continues to be a difficult task. This is due in part to the fact that many basses, like their cousins the wrasses, are highly changeable in sex and coloration. Groupers are accomplished quick-change artists,

1

adept at changing their colors to match their background. They can flash from spots to stripes, blotches, bars or solid colors as they move from coral to rock to sandy bottom. Many species show a distinct difference in color with depth. Fishes taken from deeper waters have much more red coloration. This highly developed ability to change coloration protects them from larger predators, and enables them to prey effectively on smaller fishes.

☐ Some groupers seem to change their coloration wildly at feeding time. In writing about the Indo-Pacific cerise grouper (*Variola louti*), the aquarist Graham Cox states that "when at rest, it is an uninspiring russet-brown with a hint of blue spots scattered over its body. If a small, live fish is introduced into the tank, a miraculous change in appearance occurs. Almost imperceptibly at first, then with gathering momentum, the fish's whole body becomes suffused with an indescribable shade of red. Small islets of sapphire-blue radiate a strange glow as the fish's body pulsates with light a few seconds before the 'grouper lunge.' After capturing the fish, the grouper's colors subside until the next mealtime."

Black sea bass *Centropristis striata* To 22 inches. A very popular bottom fish among sport fishermen along the Atlantic coast, from southern Massachusetts to northern Florida. Two closely related species, *C. philadelphica* (rock sea bass) and *C. ocyurus* (bank sea bass) range from South Carolina south thru the Gulf of Mexico. Although related to the striped bass, this sea bass is exclusively marine, never venturing into rivers or streams. An excellent food fish with fine, white flaky flesh. Averaging 1½ to 3 pounds it will run occasionally to 5 pounds. **Range:** southern Massachusetts to northern Florida. **Edibility:** excellent.

Nassau grouper (cherna criolla) *Epinephelus striatus* To 4 feet. This beautifully colored fish is the least wary and most friendly of all the groupers. If once offered food, it will return again and again to pester divers for handouts. It is most like the red grouper in appearance, but has much bolder stripes , a black spot or saddle at the base of the soft dorsal, and notched dorsal spines (the red groupers' dorsal is smooth). A notorious color-changer, the Nassau grouper can blend perfectly into any background, from pale white to solid black. A very important food fish in the West Indies. **Range:** North Carolina and Bermuda south to the 'hump' of Brazil, including the Gulf of Mexico. **Edibility:** good.

Speckled hind, calico grouper *Epinephelus drummondhayi* To 20 inches. Distinctive for being the only grouper covered with small white spots on the body and all fins. One of the smaller groupers, it is rather rare over its range. **Range:** Bermuda, South Carolina, and Florida, including the Gulf of Mexico. **Edibility:** good.

Snowy grouper, golden grouper, (mero, cherna) *Epinephelus niveatus* To about 2½ feet. Young are easily recognized by the pearly white dots on body. Over 15 inches, these dots begin to fade. Large adults move well offshore to 1500 feet depths and take on a coppery gold coloration with up to 18 dark stripes on the sides. **Range:** New England to southeastern Brazil, including the Gulf of Mexico. **Edibility:** good.

☐ The sexual life of the serranids is even more surprising. Some are functional hermaphrodites: certain species of *Serranus* and *Hypoplectrus* basses are both male and female at the same time. Most groupers mature first as females and produce eggs. Later in life they reverse sex to become functioning males, which then fertilize the young females. The term "grouper" is usually applied to the larger basses belonging to the genera *Epinephelus* and *Mycteroperca*. It is a misnomer, since most large sea basses live solitarily in reef holes, crevices and burrows. Serranids range in size from a few inches to 8 feet in length and 1000 pounds in weight. In the West Atlantic the largest grouper (the jewfish) attains a weight of 800 pounds. In the Indo-Pacific there have been accounts of divers being stalked and swallowed alive by giant groupers. Some groupers, especially the Nassau grouper, become quite tame after repeated contacts with divers. Some of the smaller forms of serranids and serranid allies, including the hamlets (*Hypoplectrus* species), soapfishes (Grammistidae) and fairy basslets (Grammidae) are included here, although their precise classification and even their inclusion with the serranids is not agreed upon by all ichthyologists.

Red grouper (cherna Americana, mero, cherna de vivero) *Epinephelus morio* To 3 feet. The most abundant species of the genus, this handsome grouper is heavily fished from Virginia to Texas. Easily separable from other groupers by the elevation of the second dorsal spine, and green eyes. Highly changeable in color. Can easily be mistaken for the Nassau grouper, which see. **Range:** New England and Bermuda to Brazil, including the Gulf of Mexico. **Edibility:** good.

4

Red hind (cabrilla, tofia) *Epinephelus guttatus* To 1½ feet. The common grouper of Florida, the Gulf of Mexico and the West Indies, ranging north to North Carolina. Easily hooked or speared close inshore and on offshore banks. Party boats take this fish off the bottom using large cut baits. Can be mistaken for the rock hind, but the red hind has no large black spots on the back. **Range:** Bermuda and North Carolina to Brazil, including the Gulf of Mexico. **Edibility:** good.

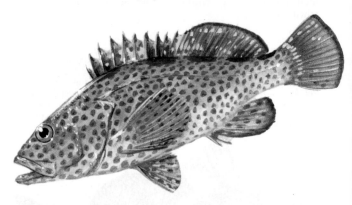

Rock hind (cabra mora, mero cabrilla) *Epinephelus adscensionis* To 1½ feet. This splendid grouper is very common in the West Atlantic. It is often seen over rocky bottoms in shallows of 10 feet of water or less. Can easily be confused with the red hind, but note the 4 to 5 large black spots along the dorsal, and the black saddle spot behind the soft dorsal. It is a more wary fish than the red hind, and more at home in inshore water turbulence. **Range:** New England and Bermuda to southeastern Brazil, including the Gulf of Mexico. **Edibility:** excellent.

Jewfish (guasa mero) *Epinephelus itajara* To 8 feet. This is the giant sea bass of the Western Atlantic. A record 7 foot jewfish was taken off Florida that weighed 680 pounds. Makes its home in large caves, coral crevices, sunken wrecks and under ledges, and when hooked, heads straight for its burrow. **Range:** Bermuda and Bahamas to southeastern Brazil, including the Gulf of Mexico. **Edibility:** excellent.

Mutton hamlet (cherna, guaseta) *Epinephelus afer* To 1 foot. A strange little seabass, closely related to the groupers, but more often a resident of sea-grass beds, rather than reef holes and crevices. Also distinctive for the stout spine on its cheek (covered by skin) possessed by no other grouper. (Previously known as *Alphestes afer.*) **Range:** Bermuda, Bahamas and Florida to Argentina. **Edibility:** good.

Warsaw grouper, black grouper (garrupa negrita, guasa mero) *Epinephelus nigritus* To 6 feet. Another monster of a grouper distinguishable from the jewfish by its brown color and its long dorsal spines (the jewfish has short dorsal spines). One of the best fighters of the groupers, usually found in deep, offshore water. Common along the Northern Gulf of Mexico. **Range:** Massachusetts to Brazil including the Gulf of Mexico. **Edibility:** good.

Marbled grouper *Epinephelus inermis* To 3 feet. A rare grouper taken occasionally off southern Florida. Said to be a secretive fish, prone to dart for reef caves and grottos when alarmed. Young are dark brown with scattered white spots. (Previously known as *Dermatolepis inermis.*) **Range:** southern Florida and the West Indies to Brazil. **Edibility:** fair.

6

Coney (guativere, corruncha) *Epinephelus fulva* To 1 foot. The coney exhibits a number of color phases, including the bi-color phase shown (thought to be an excitement phase), the golden phase, and the common phase, when the fish is a solid, dark reddish-brown. Note the two distinct spots just behind the soft dorsal and two more spots on the lower jaw, very evident in all color phases. (Previously known as *Cephalopholis fulva*.) **Range:** Bermuda, Bahamas and southern Florida to Brazil, including the Gulf of Mexico. **Edibility:** good.

Graysby (enjambre, cuna cabrilla) *Epinephelus cruentatum* To 1 foot. Another color changer capable of switching its ground color from pale white to brown, and even occasionally taking on a banded pattern not unlike the Nassau grouper. The best identifiers are the 4 or 5 distinct spots at the base of the dorsal fin. *Petrometopon cruentatum* is a synonym. **Range:** Bermuda, Bahamas and Florida to Brazil, including the Gulf of Mexico. **Edibility:** good.

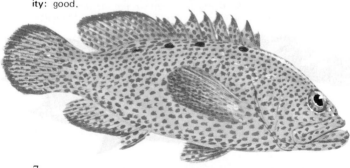

Yellowmouth grouper (abadejo) *Mycteroperca interstitialis* To 30 inches. Distinctive for its yellow mouth, faint brownish body marblings and the narrow yellow margins on virtually all fins. Popular with sport fishermen. Juveniles are sharply bi-colored—dark above and white below. **Range:** Cape Cod, Bermuda, Bahamas and Florida to Brazil. **Edibility:** good.

Scamp, salmon rockfish (abadejo, cuna garopa) *Mycteroperca phenax* To 2 feet. Though rare, the scamp is considered the finest food fish of all the groupers. Similar to the yellowmouth grouper but the brown spots on the scamp tend to run together to form hazy bands, and the fins are spotted. **Range:** Cape Cod to Florida; common in the Gulf of Mexico and in the southern Caribbean. **Edibility:** excellent.

Gag, black grouper *Mycteroperca microlepis* To 3 feet. An excellent game and table fish, the gag is distinctive for the tiger stripes radiating from the eye, and the vague, scrawled body markings. It is often taken with the red grouper along Florida coasts. Many fishermen locate grouper reefs by trolling a plug just over the bottom and tossing a buoy overboard when a gag hits the lure. **Range:** Atlantic and Gulf Coast of U.S. to Brazil. **Edibility:** excellent.

Tiger grouper (bonaci gato) *Mycteroperca tigris* To 30 inches. Easily recognized by its bold 'tiger' stripes and the trailing tags that large individuals develop on the dorsal, anal and caudal fins. Often encountered near-shore at depths from 10 to 30 feet. Like the yellowfin, the tiger grouper will rise from 50 foot depths to take a surface lure. **Range:** Bermuda, Bahamas and Florida to northern coast of Brazil, southern Gulf of Mexico. **Edibility:** good.

8

Black grouper (bonaci arara, aguají) *Mycteroperca bonaci* To 4 feet. An excellent sportfish, this grouper is notable for its size (often exceeds 50 pounds and has been reported to reach 180 pounds) and its ability to change color. It can change to a dark reddish gray, to a solid black, or it can flash to a very pale coloration. Note narrow orange margins on pectoral fins. **Range:** Massachusetts, Bermuda, Bahamas and Florida to southeastern Brazil, including the Gulf of Mexico. **Edibility:** good.

Yellowfin grouper, black grouper (bonaci de piedra, bonaci cardinal, cuna) *Mycteroperca venenosa* To 3 feet. Often confused with the closely related black grouper, the yellowfin has definite broad yellow margins on its pectoral fins. This fish is adept at changing its color, from solid black to near-red to pale green, as the background requires. **Range:** Bermuda, Bahamas and Florida to Brazil, including the Gulf of Mexico. **Edibility:** good, but large yellowfins may be toxic in ciguatera-prone areas. See page 39.

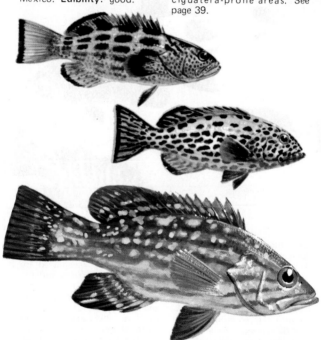

Comb grouper (cuna negra) *Mycteroperca rubra* To 30 inches. A common grouper in the southern Caribbean, this fish has bold markings when young. As the fish matures, the markings fade and become less distinct. Also, occurs in the eastern Atlantic from the Mediterranean to the Congo. **Range:** West Indies to Brazil, including the Gulf of Mexico. **Edibility:** good.

Sand perch (bolo) *Diplectrum formosum* To 1 foot. These little seabasses will excavate a burrow in the reef bottom which they use until they have outgrown it. Highly changeable in color, they can switch their pattern from vertical bars (when at rest) to longitudinal stripes (when moving). **Range:** North Carolina, Florida, the Bahamas to Uruguay, including the Gulf of Mexico. **Edibility:** good.

Lantern bass *Serranus baldwini* To 2½ inches. Often found in seagrass beds, as well as around rocks, coral rubble and shell fragments from the shoreline to 250 foot depths. Individuals from deeper water are suffused with much more red and yellow. **Range:** The Bahamas, and Florida to Surinam. **Edibility:** poor.

Chalk bass *Serranus tortugarum* To 3½ inches. A tiny, deepwater basslet, this little fish has been seen at depths from 40 to 150 feet hovering in small groups over patches of coral rubble. It has been taken at depths of 1320 feet. Appears to be a plankton feeder. **Range:** southern Florida, Bahamas and the West Indies to Honduras. **Edibility:** poor.

Harlequin bass *Serranus tigrinus* To 4 inches. This spotted beauty is a common basslet found from the shoreline out to 120 feet. Fond of seagrass beds, coral and rocks, the harlequin bass feeds mainly on crustaceans. **Range:** Bermuda, Bahamas and southern Florida to Yucatan. **Edibility:** poor.

10

Orangeback bass *Serranus annularis* To 3½ inches. This brilliant little seabass is not seen by many divers since its preferred depth range is 100 to 200 feet. It is frequently seen in pairs, swimming close to the bottom. **Range:** Bermuda, Bahamas and south Florida to Brazil. **Edibility:** poor.

Belted sandfish *Serranus subligarius* To 3 inches. Lives at moderate depths off the coasts of southern U.S. Has been taken in such varying locales as Beaufort, North Carolina, Charleston and Pensacola. This fish became famous for its reproductive powers when an isolated belted sandfish in an aquarium fertilized its own eggs. **Range:** see above. **Edibility:** poor.

Swissguard basslet, peppermint basslet *Liopropoma rubre* To 3½ inches. Unfortunately this brilliant beauty is a very shy, secretive fish, living deep in the recesses of reef caves and crevices, thus it is rarely seen by divers. When placed in an aquarium, it may be weeks before this fish will venture out of hiding. Found over a depth range from 10 to 140 feet. **Range:** Bahamas, Florida Keys to Curacao and Yucatan. **Edibility:** poor.

Candy basslet *Liopropoma carmabi* To 2 inches. Quite similar to the Swissguard basslet, and with the same, secretive habits. Note the differences in coloration and striping. Also, the candy basslet has no spot on the anal fin, and the two spots on the caudal fin lobes are clearly separated by blue lines. **Range:** Bahamas, Puerto Rico, Barbados, Bonaire and Curacao. **Edibility:** poor.

Ridgeback basslet, cave bass *Liopropoma mowbrayi* To 3¼ inches. Not previously recorded from the U.S. until W.A. Starck sighted one of these elusive cave dwellers on Alligator Reef off the Florida Keys. Lives in caves and crevices at depths of from 100 to 180 feet. **Range:** Bermuda, Bahamas, Florida Keys, Puerto Rico and Curacao. **Edibility:** poor.

Tobaccofish (guatacare de canto) *Serranus tabacarius* To 6½ inches. The light portions of this fish may vary from bright yellow to pale white. Sometimes it is suffused with rose-red tints, other times with olive. A solitary fish, it ranges from 3 to 250 feet. **Range:** Bermuda, Bahamas and south Florida and throughout the West Indies. **Edibility:** poor.

12

Butter hamlet (vaca) *Hypoplectrus unicolor* To 5 inches. The hamlets are small seabasses distinctive for their often lavish coloration, and for their deeper, foreshortened, almost snapper-like body profile. They tend to slink, catlike, about the reef in a deliberate manner, as though stalking other fishes. Even though many of the hamlets were first described by the Cuban ichthyologist Felipe Poey y Aloy in 1852, very little is known about them to date. Many of them are quite rare, and some of them are found only at 100 to 140 foot depths. The butter hamlet is quite common in the Florida Keys, and Cervigon reports that it is abundant off Western Venezuela, but it appears to be fairly rare in the Caribbean. **Range:** Bermuda, Bahamas, Florida to Brazil. **Edibility:** poor.

Blue hamlet *Hypoplectrus gemma* To 5 inches. This rare hamlet, a splendid iridescent blue animal, is so far reported only from Florida, although it is probably more widespread. Starck reports that it is common at Alligator Reef in the Florida Keys. **Range:** southern Florida. **Edibility:** poor.

Barred hamlet, banded hamlet (vaca) *Hypoplectrus puella* To 6 inches. This is the most common hamlet, often seen picking stealthily about shallow reefs, especially in the West Indies. Scientists of the Tektite II Program found it to be very common at Lameshur Bay in the Virgin Islands, and Starck lists it as "occasional" at Alligator Reef in the Florida Keys. **Range:** Bermuda, Bahamas, Florida Keys, Gulf Coast of Florida, West Indies. **Edibility:** poor.

Golden hamlet (vaca) *Hypoplectrus gummigutta* To 5 inches. Apparently a deep-water hamlet. Bohlke and Chaplin report one individual taken at 120 feet in the Exumas, Bahamas. Poey found it to be fairly common around Cuba. **Range:** Bahamas, Cuba, Jamaica, Dominican Republic. **Edibility:** poor.

14

Yellowtail hamlet *Hypoplectrus chlorurus* To 5 inches. Distinctive for its dark body with the bright yellow caudal fin. Reported from the West Indies, Venezuela, and from the southern Texas coast, where it was found around shallow, rocky wharves. **Range:** see above. **Edibility:** poor.

Shy hamlet (vaca) *Hypoplectrus guttavarius* To 5 inches. A beautiful little seabass, apparently very shy, which has been taken only in the Bahamas, Florida Keys and in scattered locales in the West Indies. Poey reported it to be fairly common off Cuba. **Range:** see above. **Edibility:** poor.

15

Yellowbelly hamlet (vaca) *Hypoplectrus aberrans* To 5 inches. So far recorded from the Florida Keys and the West Indies. Tektite II scientists observed a few of these at Lameshur Bay, Virgin Islands. **Range:** Southern Florida and the West Indies. **Edibility:** poor.

Indigo hamlet (vaca) *Hypoplectrus indigo* To 5½ inches. A blue version of the barred hamlet, so far taken from the Bahamas, Florida, Cuba, Haiti, Jamaica and off Honduras. **Range:** see above. **Edibility:** poor.

Black hamlet (vaca) *Hypoplectrus nigricans* To 6 inches. Differs from other hamlets in its dark bluish-black coloration and in the longer pelvic fins of adult fishes. Can be mistaken for a damselfish when seen on the reef. **Range:** Bahamas, Florida, West Indies. **Edibility:** poor.

16

Fairy basslet, royal gramma *Gramma loreto* To 3 inches. The fairy basslets (Grammidae family) are small, brilliantly colored allies of the groupers and seabasses. Five species are known from the tropical Western Atlantic. Two of the most attractive and best known are the fairy basslet and the blackcap basslet. Favorites of aquarists and rare fish fanciers, they are spectacular showpieces for any aquarium. The fairy basslet is usually found hiding in caves, holes or under ledges over a depth range from a few feet to 200 feet. Bohlke and Chaplin report it is common everywhere in the Bahamas. Groups of 2 or 3 to a dozen or more cluster in the same cave. **Range:** Bermuda and the Bahamas through the Caribbean to Venezuela. **Edibility:** poor.

Blackcap basslet *Gramma melacara* To 4 inches. So far known only from the Bahamas and the islands off British Honduras, this lovely magenta-hued basslet is exceedingly abundant at 100 and 200 foot depths, where it is found under overhangs and in crevices of the extremity of the offshore bank. **Range:** See above. **Edibility:** poor.

Creole fish (rabirubia de lo alto) *Paranthias furcifer* To 11 inches. A handsome, flame-colored fish which, like the creole wrasse and blue chromis, is often seen in small schools high in the water column, feeding on the tiny plankton that swarm about the reef. Note the 3 bold white spots along the back. **Range:** Bermuda and southern Florida to Brazil, including the Gulf of Mexico. **Edibility:** fair.

Greater soapfish (pez jabon) *Rypticus saponaceus* To 13 inches. The soapfishes (family Grammistidae) are small, bass-like fishes named for the suds-like mucus they produce when they are caught or handled. In some species (*Rypticus saponaceus* is one) this mucus is toxic, perhaps serving to ward off predators. **Range:** Bermuda, Bahamas and Florida to Brazil, including the Central American coast. **Edibility:** poor.

18

JACKS, POMPANOS, PERMITS, SCAD

Horse-eye jack (ojo gordo) *Caranx latus* To 2½ feet. Often confused with the crevalle jack, but easily distinguished by the large eye, black dorsal fin, yellow tail, and numerous other characteristics. Often enters fresh water. An inquisitive, bold jack, the horse-eye will approach a diver closely. Occasionally implicated in ciguatera poisoning in the West Indies. Young have 6 body bands. **Range:** New Jersey and Bermuda to southeastern Brazil, including the Gulf of Mexico. **Edibility:** good—see above.

Pound for pound the offshore jack fishes of the Carangidae family are the fastest, most voracious fishes of the sea. They are deep water fishes that range the ocean in roving predaceous schools. Frequently they will sweep in over the reefs to feed on resident fishes. Jacks depend on their speed of attack to kill. Their speed and tenacity provide a real challenge to the fisherman that hooks one. It is the toughest fighting fish for its size known. The jack will rarely break out of the water, but takes punishing runs and dives for deep water, and never gives in until it is completely exhausted. Even small juvenile 4 to 8 inch jacks are dauntless fighters.

☐ West Atlantic jacks display a wide range of body shapes and sizes. The roving offshore jacks include the moderately deep-bodied jacks of the genus *Caranx*, the amberjacks (*Seriola*), the cigar-shaped scads (*Decapterus*)

Bar jack, skip jack (cibi mancho, cojinua) *Caranx ruber* To 2 feet. The bar jack is the most common West Indian jack, frequently seen by divers over the reefs. It is a splendid fish to see underwater. In the sunlight the sky blue bar bordered by black along the dorsal fin base gleams like a ribbon of blue neon. Young to 5 inches have about 7 dark bars on body. **Range:** New Jersey south to Bermuda, Bahamas, Florida, through Antilles to Venezuela, including the Gulf of Mexico. **Edibility:** good — excellent when smoked.

Crevalle jack, common jack, cavally (caballa, jiguagua, jurel, toro) *Caranx hippos* To 3½ feet. An abundant jack, valuable as a food fish, especially in Central American markets. Smaller fishes are said to be good eating, but individuals over 1½ feet are reported to be dark and almost tasteless. A fierce, stubborn and tenacious gamefish, a 20-pounder may take an hour to land on light tackle. **Range:** Nova Scotia to Uruguay including the Gulf of Mexico. **Edibility:** see above.

and the rainbow runner (*Elagatis*). The deep-bodied and compressed pompanos, permits and palometas (*Trachinotus* and *Alectis*), and the highly-compressed and high-browed lookdowns (*Selene*) are for the most part inshore fishes that feed on mollusks, small fishes, sea urchins and crustaceans found over sand flats, reefs and mud bottoms. These fishes make excellent eating. Some of the larger offshore jacks, including the amberjack, almaco jack, yellow jack, horse-eye jack and black jack are suspected of carrying ciguatera poisoning, especially large adults of these species. Where the fish poisoning problem is serious, as in certain West Indian locales, hungry natives will not take large adults of these fishes as a gift. (See "Ciguatera Poisoning," page 39).

☐ The bar jack is one of the most common jacks, often seen by divers around inshore reefs and jetties. It schools seasonally in enormous shoals of thousands of fishes, called 'passing jack' in the Bahamas. An excellent game fish and one of the best eating of the *Caranx* jacks is the blue runner. Schools sweep in over the reefs occasionally to feed on smaller fishes, but rarely linger. The colorful amberjack is a large fighting jack that dwells well off-

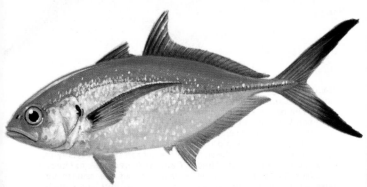

Blue runner, hard-tailed jack (atun, caballa) *Caranx fusus* To 2½ feet. This fish and the crevalle jack are the most abundant jacks of the eastern seaboard of the U.S. Also very common in the Gulf of Mexico. Divers often see them hovering singly, in pairs or pods around reefs, docks and jetties. Young have 8 vertical bands across body. Previously known as *Caranx crysos*. **Range:** Nova Scotia to southeastern Brazil, including the Gulf of Mexico. **Edibility:** good.

Yellow jack (cibi amarillo, cojinua) *Caranx bartholomaei* To 3 feet. Occasionally confused with the blue runner and bar jack, but the yellow jack is usually suffused with yellow (fins and body), lacks the spot on the gill cover of the blue runner, and has no dorsal-to-tail bar like the bar jack. Tiny ¾ inch young have 5 body bars. **Range:** New England to the hump of Brazil, including the Gulf of Mexico. **Edibility:** fair to good. A market fish in the West Indies, occasionally implicated in ciguatera poisoning.

Black jack (cibi negro) *Caranx lugubris* To 3 feet. An unusual jack in many respects, this rare fish is reported to be world-wide in tropical waters, principally from isolated or offshore islands. It is a sport fish of some importance off the Bahama Banks. **Range:** circumtropical—in the West Atlantic from Bermuda and the Bahamas to southeastern Brazil, including offshore in the Gulf of Mexico. **Edibility:** implicated in ciguatera poisoning in the West Indies and the Indo-Pacific. Larger fish are more toxic.

African pompano, Atlantic threadfin (flechudo) *Alectis crinitus* To 3 feet. Not a true pompano, this carangid is closely related to the Indo-Pacific threadfin, *Alectis ciliaris*. The illustration shows the surprising difference between a small juvenile and a large adult. So different in appearance are the two that adults were once mistakenly classed as a separate species, *Hynnis cubensis* (the "Cuban jack"). A fine game fish, usually taken by trolling.
Range: Massachusetts to Brazil, including the Gulf of Mexico.
Edibility: fair.

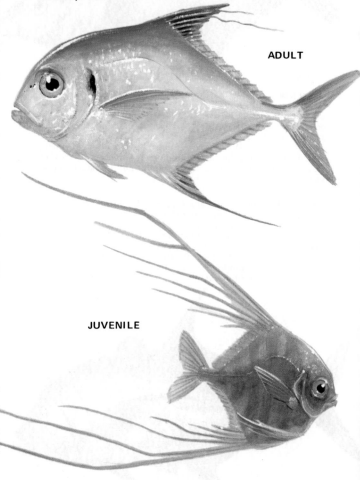

ADULT

JUVENILE

shore in fairly deep water. It sounds with speed and power and is a popular game fish. The rainbow runner is a rare but respected game fish that roams the open water. It is a solitary fish, swift and restless, that puts up a ferocious fight when hooked. As it dies, its brilliant rainbow colors fade to dull grey.

□ Permits and pompanos often root close inshore for the mollusks and crustaceans that are a major part of their diet. They are very flighty, nervous fishes, hard to hook. Anglers often despair, after seeing hundreds of permits and pompanos on a fishing trip, of landing or even hooking a single fish. The African pompano is an exotic member of the Carangidae family, with long trailing threads that stream from its dorsal and anal fins. It was once assumed that only juveniles sported the long streamers, and the threads shortened with age. Numerous adult fishes from 1½ to 2 feet long have been taken, however, with threadfins almost as long as the juveniles. Most juvenile jackfishes display bold or light vertical bars (as shown by the juvenile African pompano) which fade as the fish matures.

Florida pompano, pompano *Trachinotus carolinus* To 2½ feet. Epicures proclaim this fish to be the very finest food from either fresh or saltwater. The flesh is firm, flaky and flavorsome. An excellent gamefish on light tackle, pompanos are extremely nervous, unpredictable and panicky when stalked. Rooting close inshore for mollusks and crustaceans, they may show anglers a tail or flank, then bolt. Young are much like adults in form. Adults are very similar to the adult permit. **Range:** Massachusetts to Brazil, including the Gulf of Mexico. Most abundant off Florida and in the Gulf of Mexico. **Edibility:** see above.

24

Atlantic permit, round pompano (young) *Trachinotus falcatus*
To 3 feet, 9 inches. Young permit, previously called "round
pompano," and thought to be a separate species, are now recognized to be juveniles on their way to becoming adult permit.
The juvenile and adult phases of the fish are so dissimilar, as illustrated, that it is easy to see why they were first assumed to be
different species. Much like the pompano, the permit is the
angler's delight and agony. They are very wary, skittish fishes
that can wear down nerves by their unwillingness to take a baited
hook. It may require from 30 minutes to 3 hours to land a large
permit on light tackle. While not as succulent as the pompano,
the permit is a fine food fish. **Range:** recorded from both sides
of the Atlantic. In the west Atlantic from New England to Brazil, including the Gulf of Mexico. **Edibility:** excellent.

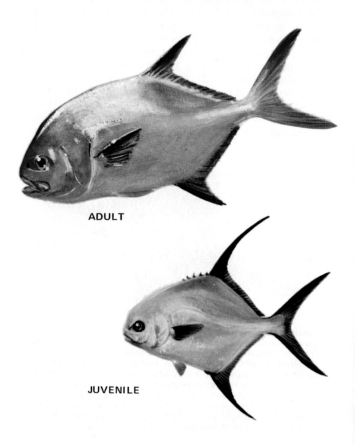

ADULT

JUVENILE

Palometa, gafftopsail pompano, longfin pompano *Trachinotus goodei* To 15 inches. This is the most graceful and striking of all the carangids. To be circled again and again by a school of 25 to 50 palometas is an exhilarating experience for a diver and one that is quite common, especially in the West Indies. It is an abundant fish in clear water along sandy, exposed shores, where it feeds on small fishes, mollusks and crustaceans. Occasionally feeds in the company of the threadfin and the sand drum. It is often confused with the young permit, but the palometa has 4 distinct bars on its side that the permit lacks, and the dorsal and anal fins are much longer than those of the permit. Long known as *T. glaucus*. **Range:** New England, Bermuda, Bahamas and Florida south to Argentina, including the Gulf of Mexico. **Edibility:** good.

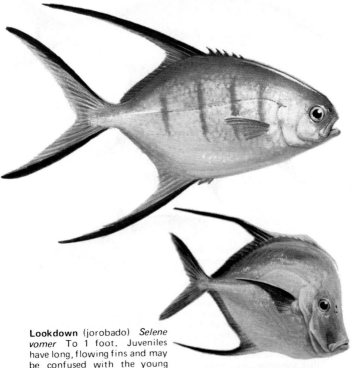

Lookdown (jorobado) *Selene vomer* To 1 foot. Juveniles have long, flowing fins and may be confused with the young African pompano, but the eye of the pompano is much closer to the mouth (one eye diameter or less) than that of the lookdown. A closely related fish, *Vomer setapinnis*, the moonfish, has the same range as the lookdown, and is quite similar in appearance. **Range:** Massachusetts and Bermuda to Uruguay, including the Gulf of Mexico. **Edibility:** excellent.

26

Greater amberjack (coronado) *Seriola dumerili* To 6 feet. This roving offshore predator is the largest and most common of the Atlantic amberjacks, and is a prime target of the charterboat fisheries of Florida, the Carolinas and the Gulf of Mexico. A record 5 foot 11 inch fish was taken from the Bahamas that weighed 149 pounds. Usually taken trolling at or near the surface, but has been taken bottom fishing at 180 feet. Two-inch young have 5 body bands, which begin to fade at 8 inches. **Range:** circumtropical; in the West Atlantic, from Massachusetts to Brazil, including the Gulf of Mexico. **Edibility:** fair, but in the West Indies is second only to the barracuda in causing ciguatera poisoning (see page 39).

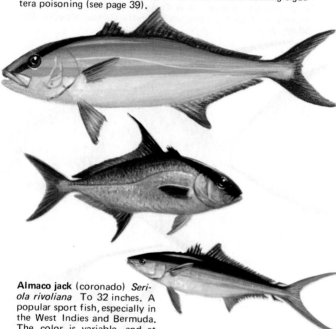

Almaco jack (coronado) *Seriola rivoliana* To 32 inches. A popular sport fish, especially in the West Indies and Bermuda. The color is variable, and at times the almaco jack appears quite like the amberjack, including a brassy stripe from nose to tail. It is a deeper-bodied fish, however, with much longer dorsal and anal fin lobes than the amberjack. Young display 5 or 6 dark body bands. Previously known as *Seriola falcata*. **Range:** New Jersey and Bermuda to Argentina, including the Gulf of Mexico. **Edibility:** fair,

Rainbow runner (salmon) *Elagatis bipinnulata* To 4 feet. A rare and wide-ranging species and an esteemed game fish when taken on light tackle. A record 3 foot 11 inch runner was taken off Hawaii. **Range:** circumtropical in warm seas. In the West Atlantic from Massachusetts to Venezuela, including the Gulf of Mexico. **Edibility:** excellent.

Leatherjacket (zapatero) *Oligoplites saurus* To 1 foot. Leatherjackets are schooling fishes usually found along sandy beaches, inlets and bays. They possess sharp dorsal and anal spines capable of inflicting injury if carelessly handled. **Range:** Massachusetts to Uruguay. **Edibility:** poor.

Mackerel scad (antonino) *Decapterus macarellus* To 1 foot. The *Decapterus* genus scads all possess a detached finlet behind both the dorsal and anal fins. The mackerel scad is an offshore fish, occasionally seen schooling over the outer reefs. Due to its small size, it is usually ignored by anglers. It is important as a bait fish either salted or frozen. **Range:** Nova Scotia to the hump of Brazil. **Edibility:** good.

Round scad (chuparaco) *Decapterus punctatus* To 1 foot. An offshore schooling fish, occasionally taken inshore in beach seines. Primarily used as a bait fish, it is not sought by anglers, although it reportedly has a good flavor and is often sold in fish markets. **Range:** Nova Scotia to Brazil, including the Gulf of Mexico. **Edibility:** good.

Bigeye scad, goggle - eye jack *Selar crumenophthalmus* To 16 inches. This scad is a popular food fish and is often found in West Indian markets. Also popular as a live bait fish. Occurs on outer reefs in large schools. **Range:** circumtropical; in the Western Atlantic, from Nova Scotia to Rio de Janeiro, including the Gulf of Mexico. **Edibility:** good.

28

TUNAS AND MACKERELS

Bluefin tuna, thon (atun azul) *Thunnus thynnus* To 14 feet. The giant of the mackerel family and among the largest of all fishes. A 1,600 pound, 14 foot tuna was taken off New Jersey. One of the world's gamest animals, it has been described as "a living meteor" when hooked. A 125 pound bluefin has been known to fight an angler for 7 hours, and tow a small boat 20 miles offshore. In the first 3 months of life the bluefin averages 13 inches and 1½ pounds. Within 14 years it will reach 105 inches and 700 pounds. Worldwide in distribution, bluefins range the West Atlantic from Newfoundland to Puerto Rico and the Gulf of Mexico. Fishes tagged off the Bahamas have been captured in Norway, indicating transatlantic migration. **Range:** see above. **Edibility:** good.

For spectacular big-game fishing, and for fishermen who don't mind hard work, a good place to be is in the Bahamas when shoals of great bluefin tuna pass in migration from early May to June 15. Schools of 200- to 800-pound tackle busters make their crossing in the shallows near the Gulf Stream dropoff. These magnificent blue-water predators are heading for their summer feeding grounds in the North Atlantic, to feed on herring off Nova Scotia, and the ling, whiting, and butterfish off the New York and New Jersey coasts. Battling a 500-pound bluefin is no job for an amateur, and spectacular struggles between man and tuna are waged in the Bahama shallows. Smaller but no less fascinating struggles are waged throughout the Gulf of Mexico, the east coast of the U.S., Bermuda, and throughout the Carribbean with other fighting representatives of the Scombridae, the tunas and mackerels.

Yellowfin tuna, Allison's tuna (atun) *Thunnus albacares* To 7 feet. Although some sport fishermen still insist that Allison's tuna is a distinct species, fishery biologists have concluded that the large tuna with very long, trailing yellow dorsal and anal fins are merely adult specimens of the well-known yellowfin tuna of both the Atlantic and Pacific. Splendid gamefishes, they are sought by anglers in the West Indies and the Gulf of Mexico north to Maryland and New Jersey. They average 20 to 120 pounds. The largest yellowfin, taken in Hawaii, was 6 feet, 10½ inches, weighing 266½ pounds. **Range:** world-wide in tropical waters. In the West Atlantic, from New England to the Gulf of Mexico, and throughout the Caribbean to Brazil. **Edibility:** good.

☐ The scombrids are fork-tailed, heavily-muscled fishes built for a roving, predaceous existence at the ocean's surface. They prey on smaller fishes, and tuna-wise boat captains keep their eyes peeled for the flocks of screaming, diving sea birds which feed upon the smaller fishes and squid driven to the surface by the pursuing tuna. When a school is sighted, the captain runs the boat across the head of the school, slows to a few knots, and live anchovies and other tuna bait fish are thrown overboard to keep the tuna circling.

☐ All of the tunas and most of the mackerels are popular shore and offshore game fish because they are very fast swimmers that strike hard and pull hard, preferring to run and sound down deep, rather than to twist and battle the hook. The thrill of tuna fishing is the long drawn out battle of sheer weight. Frequently the fisherman never sees the fish until it is hauled up, completely exhausted, alongside the boat. The little tuna, bonito, skipjack and blackfin tuna are small tuna favorites of West Atlantic

30

fishermen for their splendid fighting qualities and food value. Another favorite in the big game fish class is the yellowfin tuna, a magnificent fighter that reaches 300 pounds in weight, although the average taken is 40 to 50 pounds.

□ The wahoo is a long, slender mackerel also known for its fighting prowess. Acclaimed for its excellent flavor, the wahoo is a circumtropical fish, taken throughout the Caribbean and Gulf of Mexico. The king mackerel is a prime favorite of West Atlantic offshore fishermen. The king is a voracious feeder and will hit a trolled bait with considerable shock and power. Kings run the year around in Florida, with the biggest runs coming to southern Florida in the winter months. In Texas, Louisiana and Mississippi waters, kings run in the late spring and throughout the summer. The Spanish mackerel and cero are excellent food fishes, targets of shore and offshore fishermen from Florida to Texas, and from Massachusetts to Rio de Janeiro. Experienced gulf coast fishermen say that the Spanish mackerels will run when gulf water temperature reaches 75° or more. These runs hit Texas waters around Easter Week each year and continue to run along Texas, Louisiana and Mississippi waters for about five

Albacore, longfin tuna (albacora, atun) *Thunnus alalunga* To 4 feet. Rare in the West Atlantic, except for the Bahamas and Cuba, the long-finned albacore is occasionally taken by sport fishermen well offshore. A popular gamefish reaching 90 pounds in weight. The average caught is about 20 pounds. The most valuable of all the tunas for canning, and the only one that can be labeled as "white meat tuna." **Range:** world-wide in all tropical seas; in the West Atlantic from New Jersey to Puerto Rico, including the Gulf of Mexico. **Edibility:** excellent.

31

months. Spanish mackerels and ceros are caught from beachfront piers and jetties, and occasionally even by surf casting. More frequently, however, they are caught a few miles offshore, particularly where swirling currents carry small fishes away from the protection of coral and rock reefs. Tunas and mackerels are excellent eating when fresh, but the oily meat deteriorates very quickly in tropical heat. Always drain the blood away immediately after landing—preferably into a bucket, and not overboard (unless you want a school of sharks on your trail). Freezing these fishes is not recommended, due to the high oil content. They should be eaten fresh. Cases of food poisoning in the tropics are common from eating spoiled tuna and mackerel.

Blackfin tuna (albacora) *Thunnus atlanticus* To 3 feet. A small dark-colored species, the blackfin is an excellent food fish, and many are taken in Cuba's commercial fishery. Commonly hooked by offshore anglers in Florida and the West Indies. A favorite food of the blue marlin. **Range:** Cape Cod to Brazil. **Edibility:** good.

Atlantic bonito, little tunny (bonite) *Sarda sarda* To 3 feet. Huge, voracious schools roam the West Atlantic, hot in pursuit of squid, mackerels, menhaden, and alewives. Anglers looking for bigger game find that even 4 to 8 pound bonito are furious fighters. Often called "skip jacks" and "horse mackerels." **Range:** St. Lawrence River to Argentina, including the Gulf of Mexico. **Edibility:** poor.

32

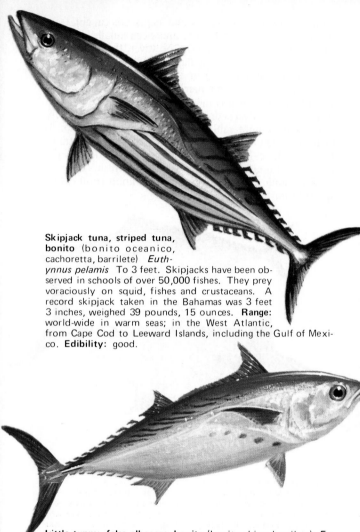

Skipjack tuna, striped tuna, bonito (bonito oceanico, cachoretta, barrilete) *Euthynnus pelamis* To 3 feet. Skipjacks have been observed in schools of over 50,000 fishes. They prey voraciously on squid, fishes and crustaceans. A record skipjack taken in the Bahamas was 3 feet 3 inches, weighed 39 pounds, 15 ounces. **Range:** world-wide in warm seas; in the West Atlantic, from Cape Cod to Leeward Islands, including the Gulf of Mexico. **Edibility:** good.

Little tunny, false albacore, bonito (bonito chico, barrilete) *Euthynnus alletteratus* To 4 feet. Popular east coast and Gulf Coast sport fishes; anglers gear up for the little tuna in summer and fall, when schools are abundant around inlets, bays and beaches. The average taken is 5 to 8 pounds, and rare 35 pounders have been recorded. An important West Indian market fish. **Range:** New England, Bermuda, Bahamas to Brazil. **Edibility:** good.

Spanish mackerel (caballa, sierra) *Scomberomorus maculatus*
To 4 feet. When a silvery, gold-spotted projectile grabs a trolled
bait from a Florida charter boat and then leaps 10 feet into the
air to begin a furious fight, the fish is a Spanish mackerel. Commercial fishermen use aircraft to spot schools off Florida and
the Gulf and take nearly 10 million pounds per year. Menhaden
are their favorite food. **Range:** Maine to Brazil, including the
Gulf of Mexico. **Edibility:** excellent.

Cero, painted mackerel (caballa, pintada, sierra) *Scomberomorus
regalis* To 3½ feet. Another splendid leaper and fighter, the cero
is often confused with the Spanish mackerel. The two very similar mackerels can be distinguished by the body markings. The
cero has a series of dot-and-dashed gold lines from pectoral fin
to tail while the Spanish mackerel has large definite spots from
pectoral fin to tail. A beautiful fish, occasionally appearing in
large schools off Florida and through the West Indies. **Range:**
Cape Cod to Brazil, including the Gulf of Mexico. **Edibility:**
good.

King mackerel, kingfish (carite, sierra conalera, caballa) *Scomberomorus cavalla* To 5 feet. The largest of the Spanish mackerels, this magnificent fish may vault out of the sea when hooked and leap 25 feet in the air before starting a long, furious battle. Anglers use trolled spoons, fish and squid to land these fighters. At times, more than 100 boats may be concentrated over a large school of kings. **Range:** North Carolina to Brazil, including the Gulf of Mexico. **Edibility:** good.

Frigate mackerel *Auxis thazard* To 2½ feet. Like the little tuna, this fish may school inshore in summer and fall, but its appearance is irregular. It is not highly valued as food, but is often used as bait. Averaging one to three pounds, it can reach 10 pounds. **Range:** world-wide; in the West Atlantic, from Cape Cod to Brazil. **Edibility:** poor.

Wahoo (peto, bonito negro) *Acanthocybium solanderi* To 7 feet. This famous fighter takes off so fast on its initial run that light tackle fishermen must pursue it full throttle to prevent their lines from being stripped. If it can be checked, the wahoo provides a breathtaking battle of 30 foot leaps, soundings and long runs. Rare over its range, the wahoo often swims solitarily about Florida and West Indian reefs and in blue water. **Range:** all tropical seas; in the West Atlantic, from Maryland to Venezuela, including the Gulf of Mexico. **Edibility:** excellent.

35

SNAPPERS

Gray snapper, mangrove snapper (pargo prieto, caballerote) *Lutjanus griseus* To 2½ feet. Like most of the lutjanids, the gray snapper is highly changeable in color—sometimes very pale, sometimes very dark, often tinged with red or olive, sometimes covered with bars or blotches. The broad oblique stripe through the eye, like that of the schoolmaster, is usually apparent, but not always. Common inshore in such habitats as coral reefs, rocky outcroppings, piers, and wrecks. Especially fond of mangrove sloughs, earning the name "mangrove snapper." **Range:** Massachusetts south to Bermuda, Florida and the Bahamas to southeastern Brazil, including the Gulf of Mexico. **Edibility:** excellent.

Snappers are well-known for their excellent food quality. They are sought after by every manner of fisherman's bait and underwater spear technique. Probably because of this popularity, snappers are the wariest of game fishes. Many West Atlantic fishermen swear that snappers not only are able to think, but can even out-think the fisherman. Because of this wariness, and because of their preference for the deeper reefs, large snappers are not often seen by the casual diver. Smaller representatives of many species, especially the schoolmaster, mahogany and yellowtail snappers, are common off most shallow reefs.

☐ The carnivorous snappers of the Lutjanidae family are closely related to the grunts. Both have the characteristic sloping head and shovel-nosed appearance known as the "snapper look." Although primarily marine in habitat, some lutjanids, such as the dog and gray snappers, readily enter brackish and fresh water. Snappers are numerous in the headwater springs of the Homosassa and other rivers along Florida's west coast. Shallow mangrove areas provide ideal nursery grounds for many snappers. Although most of the lutjanids shown here are shore snappers, a few, such as the red, blackfin and silk snappers are deep‑water fishes. These and a few other closely‑

Schoolmaster (pargo amarillo, caji) *Lutjanus apodus* To 2 feet. The commonest and most familiar snapper on tropical West Atlantic reefs. The schoolmaster is virtually everywhere—coral reefs, particularly elkhorn coral stands, rocky bottoms, tide pools, turtle grass, marl and mangrove-lined tidal creeks. Juveniles are brilliantly striped in yellow like bumble bees. **Range:** New England, Bermuda, Bahamas, and Florida to Brazil, including the Gulf of Mexico. **Edibility:** good.

Mutton snapper (pargo, pargo criollo, sama) *Lutjanus analis* To 30 inches. A very handsome snapper, distinctive for its reddish fins, blue markings around the eye and the bold spot beneath the soft dorsal fin. Can be confused with the mahogany snapper underwater, but the mahogany lacks the grayish-green barred markings found on the sides of the mutton snapper. Prefers protected bays, tidal creeks, bights, and mangrove sloughs, where it feeds on fishes (especially small grunts) and crustaceans. **Range:** Massachusetts south to the Bahamas and Florida to Brazil, including the Gulf of Mexico. **Edibility:** excellent.

37

related species are the magnificent food fishes that populate the well-known "snapper banks" of the Gulf of Mexico. The banks lie in water up to 800 feet in depth. The Pensacola area is rich in snapper banks, as is the Texas

Lane snapper (biajaiba, manchego, raiado) *Lutjanus synagris* To 15 inches. A splendid fish with about 8 golden stripes running from nose to tail. Like the mutton snapper, has a subdorsal blotch, but it is hazy and less distinct. Note yellow anal and ventral fins and light olive vertical body bars. **Range:** Carolinas, Bermuda, Bahamas and Florida to southeastern Brazil, including the Gulf of Mexico. **Edibility:** excellent.

Dog snapper (jocu, pargo colorado) *Lutjanus jocu* To 3 feet. The pale triangle under the eye is distinctive. Not common anywhere, the dog snapper (named for the enlarged fang-like teeth at front of upper jaw) is found around deep reefs, submerged wreckage and rocky inshore areas. Often taken around Key West, Florida in fall and winter. **Range:** New England to Brazil, including the Gulf of Mexico. **Edibility:** good, but large dog snappers in certain areas may carry ciguatera poison. Check with local fishermen.

38

coast and Florida's east coast, especially St. Augustine and Cape Canaveral. Most snappers feed heavily on crustaceans. The large species, such as the cubera and dog snappers, are fish-eating carnivores, and are occasionally implicated in ciguatera fish poisoning.

CIGUATERA FISH POISONING

While quite rare, ciguatera is a particularly unpleasant type of food poisoning to be avoided at all costs. In certain areas at certain seasons of the year, ciguatera has been detected in such carnivores, herbivores and detritus feeders as snappers, barracuda, certain species of surgeons, groupers, jacks and moray eels. Frequently larger individuals are found to be toxic, especially barracuda, jacks and cubera and dog snappers, while smaller fishes of the same species are free of ciguatera. In the Bahamas and through the West Indies, fishes on the steep windward side of a small island may be highly toxic, while those of the same species on the shallow leeward side are perfectly edible. The first symptom is usually a tingling feeling of the mouth, lips and throat, occurring in from 1 to 30 hours after the fish is eaten. Extreme weakness, muscular pains, aches, nausea and diarrhea may follow. A mortality rate of 7 percent has been reported. If you are fishing in a strange area, and you catch and plan to eat any of the fishes named above, check first with the local population, especially local fishermen, as to the edibility of the fish. In most cases and in most areas throughout the West Atlantic, the fishes will be perfectly safe to eat.

Cubera snapper (cubera) *Lutjanus cyanopterus* To 3½ feet. Said to reach weights of 100 pounds, this is the largest of all the snappers. A very strong fighter, it is taken along submarine ledges off Cuba and Florida in 60 to 120 foot depths. **Range:** New England to the hump of Brazil, including the Gulf of Mexico. **Edibility:** good, but large individuals in certain areas may carry ciguatera toxin. Check with local fishermen.

Mahogany snapper (ojanco) *Lutjanus mahogoni* To 15 inches. Appears to the diver as a pale, almost white snapper with a distinct black subdorsal blotch. As on the mutton snapper, this blotch tends to be large on young fishes, smaller on large adults. Found in small aggregations around coral reefs and over rocky bottoms. **Range:** Carolinas and Bahamas to Venezuela. **Edibility:** excellent.

Red snapper (pargo guachinango, pargo colorado) *Lutjanus campechanus* To 30 inches. So popular and succulent is this fish that it is marketed whole, head and all, to insure against substitution. Fishes that have often been "disguised" and sold as red snapper include gray, blackfin and silk snappers, red groupers, yellowfin and black grouper, gag, scamp, snook and doubtless many others. Occurs in vast schools over deep snapper banks. Twelve million pounds of red snapper are caught on handlines each year. Juveniles to 1 foot have a subdorsal spot, which fades on adults. This is the *Lutjanus blackfordi* and *Lutjanus aya* of previous literature. **Range:** Cape Hatteras south to Yucatan, including the Gulf of Mexico. **Edibility:** excellent.

Silk snapper (pargo de lo alto) *Lutjanus vivanus* To 30 inches. Another deep water snapper, very common on snapper banks (200 to 800 foot depths) of the Gulf Stream and the Gulf of Mexico. Often confused with the red snapper, but easily distinguished by its bright yellow eye, deeply forked tail, and yellowish body lines and markings. Silk snappers up to 1 foot have a black subdorsal spot like the mutton snapper, but this disappears as the fish matures. **Range:** Carolinas, Bermuda, and Bahamas to Venezuela, including the Gulf of Mexico. **Edibility:** excellent.

Blackfin snapper (sesi, sesi de lo alto) *Lutjanus buccanella* To 20 inches. A moderately deep water snapper, usually taken from 120 to 400 foot depths. The only snapper with a distinct black blotch at the pectoral fin base. Quite common around Cuba. Juveniles are frequently seen at 20 to 60 foot depths. **Range:** Carolinas and Bermuda south to Venezuela, including the Gulf of Mexico. **Edibility:** good.

41

Vermilion snapper (cagon)
Rhomboplites aurorubens To
20 inches. A common snapper
on deeper reefs and over hard
bottoms, often caught with the
red snapper on the snapper
banks of the Gulf of Mexico at
90 to 200 foot depths. **Range:**
Carolinas, Bermuda and Bahamas to southeastern Brazil, including the Gulf of Mexico.
Edibility: excellent.

Yellowtail snapper (rabirubia)
Ocyurus chrysurus To 30
inches. In a class by itself, the
yellowtail snapper is a lovely,
active fish to see in its yellow
and blue attire, a fine fish to
catch with tenacious fighting
ability, and an excellent fish to
eat. A common snapper that
prefers open water over the top
of the reef. Usually feeds at
night on small fishes, benthic
crustaceans and plankton.
Range: New England, Bermuda, Bahamas and Florida south
to Brazil, including the Gulf of
Mexico. **Edibility:** excellent.

Black snapper (arnillo) *Apsilus dentatus* To 18 inches. A handsome dusky black snapper with a violet tinge. Even the inside of
the mouth is black. A deep water, offshore fish said to be common and a good market fish around Cuba. Recently reported
from U.S. coasts; Starck states that it is "rare, offshore," at Alligator Reef in the Florida Keys. **Range:** Bahamas, Florida through
the West Indies. **Edibility:** good.

GRUNTS

White grunt (ronco arara, corocoro) *Haemulon plumieri* To 18 inches. A lovely fish, probably the commonest and most important food fish of all the West Atlantic grunts. May be seen in dense aggregations by day at the edges of patch reefs and over any suitable bottom, usually in 20 feet or less of water. The inside of the mouth is blood-red. Engages in "kissing" displays. Distinguishable from the French and blue-striped grunt by the striped head and checked scale pattern on body. Coloration is changeable with a broad, dusky bar sometimes visible on midside of body, sometimes not. **Range:** Chesapeake Bay, Virginia, Bermuda, Bahamas, Florida and Gulf of Mexico to Brazil. **Edibility:** excellent.

In spite of their unlovely name, many of the West Atlantic grunts are brilliant, gold-striped, shimmering fishes. Grunts are virtually everywhere off Florida, Bahaman and Caribbean reefs, hovering in small groups or massing in great schools. Large schools of French, smallmouth or bluestriped grunts are often seen to stream like a river of gold between coral heads, and even a small school of cottonwicks, white grunts or porkfishes is a joy to behold. Closely related to the snappers, the grunts are also noted for their excellence as food fishes. Early settlers in the Florida Keys virtually subsisted on a diet of "grits and grunts," and today they still form an important part of the fisherman's catch. Although generally considered small panfish, many grunts attain one and a half feet (Spanish, bluestripe, white grunts) and two feet (margate and black margate) in length.

☐ Grunts, of the family Pomadasyidae, are so named because of the sounds they produce by grinding their pharyngeal teeth together. The adjacent air bladder amplifies the sound, and agitated grunts can be quite noisy when they are taken from the water. Most grunts have mouths that are bright orange-red on the inside. Certain of these (the French, white and bluestriped grunts) are known for their unique "kissing" behavior, where two grunts will face and push each other with open mouths. Hans Fricke theorizes that, like the purplemouth moray which opens its brilliantly-colored mouth to ward off aggressors, red-mouthed grunts utilize the same technique to frighten off other grunts who threaten their territory. The young of most of the grunts shown here all look very much alike, with black lateral stripes and a black spot at the base of the caudal fin, as shown for the French grunt, porkfish and black margate.

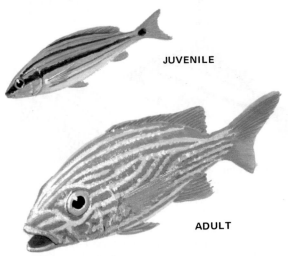

JUVENILE

ADULT

French grunt (condenado, corocoro) *Haemulon flavolineatum*
To 12 inches. Another very common grunt, beautifully marked and highly visible gathered into large, shimmering aggregations by day, often by the thousands. At night they range out over sand and grass flats to feed on benthic invertebrates. Mouth red. Engages in "kissing" displays. Swims occasionally with the white grunt. **Range:** Bermuda and South Carolina to Brazil, including the Gulf of Mexico. **Edibility:** excellent.

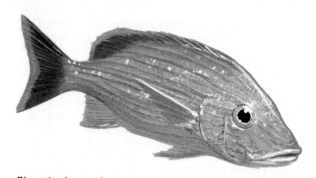

Bluestriped grunt (ronco amarillo, corocoro) *Haemulon sciurus* To 18 inches. Although it appears similar to the white and French grunts when seen on the reef, the bluestripe is distinctive for its bold blue and gold stripes on head and body, and its dusky soft dorsal and caudal fins. Often encountered swimming with the white grunt. Mouth red. Engages in "kissing" displays. A common grunt on Florida and West Indian reefs. **Range:** Bermuda and South Carolina to southeastern Brazil, including the Gulf of Mexico. **Edibility:** good.

Margate, white margate, sailor's choice (ronco blanco, jallao) *Haemulon album* To 26 inches. This excellent food fish, the largest of the grunts was named after the English seaport by early Bahaman settlers who came from Margate. Frequently seen in small groups around low corals, gorgonians, rocky areas and shipwrecks. The adult color phase is shown here. Also has a subadult color phase with no stripes, body pearly gray, soft dorsal and caudal fins black. **Range:** Bermuda, Bahamas, south Florida to Brazil. **Edibility:** excellent.

Smallmouth grunt (arara) *Haemulon chrysargyreum* To 9 inches. A reef-dwelling grunt often seen in small aggregations by day hugging the reef. At night, like other grunts, it may forage hundreds of yards from reef shelter. The mouth is red. Feeds on copepods, amphipods, ostracods and shrimps. Quite similar to the striped grunt, but the smallmouth grunt has all yellow fins and bolder body bars. **Range:** Bahamas and Florida south to Brazil. **Edibility:** fair.

Cottonwick (jeniguana) *Haemulon melanurum* To 12 inches. Not a common fish but a handsome sight to see because of its bold, scissor-like dorsal and tail stripes and the bandit-like mask which usually conceals the eye. Some fishes lack the eye stripe. The cottonwick shuns murky water, and seeks clear water, both inshore and offshore. Inside of mouth is red. **Range:** Bermuda, Bahamas, and south Florida to Brazil. **Edibility:** fair.

Sailor's choice (ronco blanco, corocoro) *Haemulon parrai* To 14 inches. Similar to the margate, but with a more distinct scale pattern accentuated by spots, and a larger eye. Feeds largely at night, taking small fishes and mollusks. Juveniles are common inshore over grass beds; adults move offshore to school in open areas of the reef. **Range:** Bahamas, south Florida to Brazil. **Edibility:** excellent.

Caesar grunt (ronco carbonero) *Haemulon carbonarium* To 15 inches. Another reef-dweller, often seen in small schools near coral heads and rocky areas. Similar to the bluestriped grunt under water, but lacks blue stripes and all fins are dusky. Mouth pale red. **Range:** Bermuda, Bahamas and south Florida to Brazil. **Edibility:** good.

Tomtate (jeniguano, cuji) *Haemulon aurolineatum* To 10 inches. One of the slimmest and smallest of the grunts, fond of schooling over sea grass and sand flats at relatively shallow depths (30 feet or less). Easily identified by the two yellow stripes on the side and the black blotch at the base of the tail. Although most juvenile grunts have a black spot at the tail base, the tomtate is one of the few that retains this blotch into adulthood. Mouth is red inside. **Range:** Cape Cod, Massachusetts, Bermuda, Bahamas, Florida, and the Gulf of Mexico south to Brazil. **Edibility:** fair.

Black grunt (ronco prieto, corocoro) *Haemulon bonariense* To 11 inches. Quite like the sailor's choice, but with the spots on the scales arranged into oblique stripes running across the body. Also note all-white fins and black tail. A rover, it is found around coral reefs, seagrass and algae beds and mud bottoms. **Range:** southern Gulf of Mexico and Cuba to Brazil. Rare in West Indies but common in the southern Caribbean. **Edibility:** good.

Spanish grunt (corocoro) *Haemulon macrostomum* To 17 inches. Much like the caesar grunt, but distinctive for the bold, dark stripes running from head to tail. The mid-lateral stripe from eye to tail is especially visible. Also note dusky belly, yellow pectoral fins, yellow-tinged caudal, dorsal and anal fins. Mature adults average about 1 foot in length. Inside of mouth is red. A bottom feeder, it prefers clear water around coral reefs. **Range:** Florida Keys south through West Indies to Brazil. **Edibility:** excellent.

Latin grunt (ronco raiado, chere-chere) *Haemulon steindachneri* To 10½ inches. Well-named for its latin distribution, this grunt occurs on both coasts of tropical America from the Gulf of California to Panama, and in the Atlantic from Santa Lucia to Brazil. Quite common on the Brazilian coast and in the southern Caribbean, though rare through the West Indies. Said to be extremely abundant around Mazatlan, Mexico. **Range:** see above. **Edibility:** good.

Striped grunt (ronco) *Haemulon striatum* To 11 inches. At one time thought to be quite rare, but now recognized to be a grunt with a preference for moderately deep water (over 40 feet). Walter Starck reports it to be abundant at Alligator Reef in the Florida Keys. Juveniles have a single mid-lateral stripe running from the eye to a dark blotch at the base of the tail. **Range:** Bahamas, Florida and Gulf of Mexico south to Brazil. **Edibility:** fair.

Porkfish (sisi, catalineta) *Anisotremus virginicus* To 14 inches. A brilliant, handsome grunt, not at all common over its range. It is rare in the Bahamas and was finally introduced to Bermuda. Abundant around Florida, especially the Keys, and has been photographed there in large magnificent schools, occasionally swimming with the white grunt. Young porkfishes pick parasites from the bodies of other fishes. **Range:** Bermuda (introduced), Bahamas, and Florida south to Brazil. **Edibility:** good.

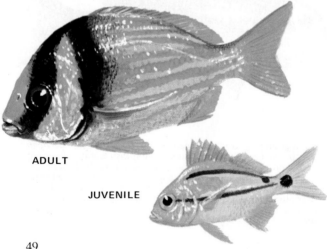

ADULT

JUVENILE

Black margate (pompon) *Anisotremus surinamensis* To 2 feet. The margates are the largest of the grunts. This fish is often seen either solitary or in small groups of 2 or 3. Favors inshore rocky bottoms, caves or the larger patch reefs where it feeds on crustaceans, fishes and sea urchins. **Range:** Florida, Bahamas, Gulf of Mexico south to Brazil. **Edibility:** good.

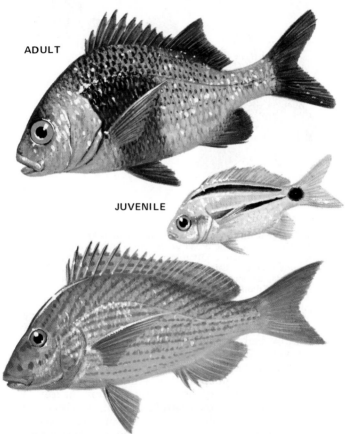

ADULT

JUVENILE

Pigfish, hogfish, sailor's choice *Orthopristis chrysoptera* To 15 inches. Ranging from Long Island south to Bermuda, Florida and through the Gulf of Mexico to the Rio Grande, the pigfish is a popular game fish and an excellent pan fish. Large numbers are taken along the Carolina coast. The *Orthopristis* genus grunts differ from the *Haemulon* grunts in their smaller mouths, more developed anal fins and less-developed dorsal spines. **Range:** see above. **Edibility:** good.

GOATFISHES

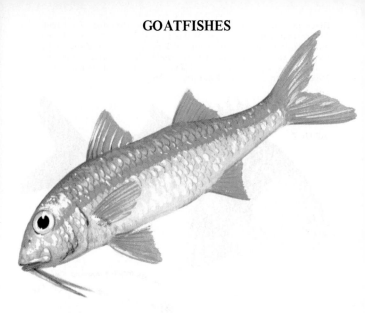

Yellow goatfish (salmonete amarillo) *Mulloidichthys martinicus*
To 15½ inches. The broad yellow stripe from eye to tail is al-
most always evident. Often seen swimming lazily in huge aggre-
gations over the reefs. Appears to be a night feeder. **Range:**
Bermuda, Bahamas and Florida to Brazil, including the Gulf of
Mexico. **Edibility:** good.

Goatfishes are the bottom grubbers of the reef, and their
distinctive characteristic is their long, tactile and highly
sensitive barbels under the chin, with which they work
constantly and busily over the bottom, probing for small
crustaceans and worms. They frequently work alone,
other times in groups of 2 or 4, other times they form
into great schools for short migrations across the reef. A
vast school of yellow goatfishes is a many-splendored
sight to see, like a shimmering curtain of gold. Goats are
very welcome sights to fishermen too, since they are excellent food fishes. The ritual spawning of goatfishes is
typical of the process of birth on the reef. A pair of goatfishes will swim together in steep loop-the-loop circles up
to the surface of the water, discharging sperm and eggs
as they ascend. If the male ejects too soon, or the female
ejects a fraction of a second too late, thousands of eggs

Spotted goatfish (salmonete colorado) *Pseudupeneus maculatus*
To 11 inches. Distinctive for the 3 large blotches on the body,
but this fish is a color-changer. When swimming the blotches
may disappear from the fish, then re-appear when settling to the
bottom. This is the goatfish usually seen rooting about sand and
mud bottoms for the invertebrates that are its main source of
food. Wrasses, rays and other fishes often follow the rooting
goatfish, to snap up morsels missed in the search. **Range:** New
England to Bermuda, the Bahamas and Florida south to Brazil,
including the Gulf of Mexico. **Edibility:** good.

perish. Although generally most eggs are fertilized, only
a small portion of the fry ever reach maturity. They are
quickly consumed by larger fishes. Many West Atlantic
fishes mate in the same way. Each of them must produce
hundreds of thousands of eggs, simply to assure that
enough are fertilized and mature to continue the species.
The eggs and fry are not wasted however. They become
part of the plankton mass which feeds other creatures of
the reef, thus assuring the survival of all species. Goats
are also noted for their ability to change color to match
their background. There is a surprising difference between their daytime and nighttime colorations. Goatfishes are members of the Mullidae family, and they are
surmullets, not to be confused with the true mullets,
which belong to the Mugilidae family.

DRUMS, CROAKERS, SEATROUT, WEAKFISHES

Weakfish, spotted sea trout, squeteague (corvina) *Cynoscion nebulosus* To 2½ feet. More U.S. anglers seek weakfish on both the Atlantic and Gulf coasts than any other sport fish. Called weakfish because the mouth and flesh are tender, they gamely respond to trolling, casting and stillfishing. Two closely related species range from Texas to Florida (*C. nebulosus*) and from Florida to Nova Scotia (*C. regalis*). Average 3 pounds; reach 15 pounds. **Range:** see above. **Edibility:** good.

Drums, croakers, roncadores, corvinas, redfishes, channel bass, seatrouts, squeteagues, weakfishes, spots, lafayettes, kingfishes, whitings—members of the large and varied family Sciaenidae are called by many names, but nearly all of them share a common characteristic—they are the noisiest fishes of the sea. Early submarine commanders were at first astounded to hear the "boop-boop-boop-boop" of schools of croakers, suspecting that enemy craft were near. Later they found they could hide the sound of their own engines behind the din of the croakers. In Chesapeake Bay, an important spawning area, the croaker cacophony begins to increase in the evening, reaches a crescendo of sound before midnight, then tapers off to near silence. Their message, if any, is still understood only by other croakers, but it is theorized that it plays an important part in courtship activity. The sound is made by vibrating special muscles attached to the air bladder, which amplifies the sound much like a guitar when a string is plucked. A few sciaenids lack air bladders (kingfishes, whitings) but they are able to produce sound by grinding their teeth together.

□ Croakers and drums are dear to the hearts of shore fishermen. They frequent warm turbid bays and estuaries—easily accessible to anglers—where they browse for shrimps, oysters, crabs and other crustaceans. Most of

Silver seatrout, silver trout, squeteague (corvina) *Cynoscion nothus* To 12 inches. Occurring from Chesapeake Bay to Florida and throughout the Gulf of Mexico, this small seatrout is related to the weakfish. It prefers open ocean more than its relatives, moving into shore in the winter months. A similar relative, the sand seatrout (*C. arenarius*) ranges from Florida's west coast to Texas and south to Mexico's Gulf of Campeche. **Range:** see above. **Edibility:** good.

Southern kingfish, whiting (corvina, lambe) *Menticirrhus americanus* To 15 inches. Occasionally divers will see this handsome, silvery fish resting or feeding on sand bottoms, quite near shore. Surfcasters bait with shrimp and hook them off sandy beaches. Four similar species range the Atlantic and Gulf coasts of the U.S. The southern kingfish *M. americanus* ranges from New York to Argentina and to the Northern Gulf of Mexico. The northern kingfish, *M. saxatilis* occurs from Maine to Florida. The Gulf kingfish, *M. littoralis* extends from Virginia to Florida and through the Gulf of Mexico. The minkfish, *M. focaliger* is restricted to the Gulf of Mexico. **Range:** see above. **Edibility:** good.

them make excellent eating and many wage a dogged struggle once they are hooked.

☐ Sciaenids are easily recognized by their two separate dorsal fins, two anal spines and a rounded snout. Also, the lateral line extends out onto the caudal fin, as in the snooks. Some croakers have barbels on the chin with which they probe sandy bottoms for crustaceans, worms and mollusks. Divers do not often encounter croakers due to their preference for sedimentary bottoms and turbid, brackish water. Occasionally a solitary, silvery black mottled kingfish is found resting on the bottom, and various drums may be seen probing the sand with their barbels.

☐ The fishes of this family are largely restricted to continental coastlines, with very few species reaching islands. With a few exceptions, none of the drums and croakers shown here are found around the islands of the West Indies, and this is true the world over. The smaller and more remote an island is from the mainland, the less like-

Red drum, channel bass, redfish (pescado colorado) *Sciaenops ocellata* To 4½ feet. Favorite of surf fishermen, the red drum swims with the weakfish, striped bass and bluefish in a hard-fighting team that attracts anglers from New Jersey to Texas. Four to six pound red drums are good eating, but over 15 pounds the flesh is coarse and stringy. Rod and reel record: 83 pounds. **Range:** Cape Cod to Florida and across the Gulf of Mexico to Texas. **Edibility:** see above.

Black drum (roncador, corvina negra) *Pogonius cromis* To 4½ feet. One of the largest food fishes on our coast; a 146 pound black drum was taken at St. Augustine, Florida. Sluggish fishes, they browse lazily in coastal shallows, probing with their sensitive barbels for crustaceans and mollusks. The loudest of the drummers, both males and females drum raucously, especially at spawning time. **Range:** Massachusetts to Argentina, including the Gulf of Mexico. **Edibility:** fair.

Silver perch *Bairdiella chrysura* To 1 foot. Fond of bays and estuaries, the silver perch is an excellent panfish (though small, averaging ¼ pound) and schoolboys and shore anglers from New Jersey to Texas fish for them actively. They are superabundant in Chesapeake Bay. Bottom fishing with small shrimp, clam, or worm is most effective. Most active in summer. **Range:** Cape Cod to Texas. **Edibility:** good.

Sand drum (petota) *Umbrina coroides* To 1 foot. One of the few drums that ranges from the U.S. coast through the West Indies to South America. Favors sandy beaches in shallow water where it swims with mojarras, palometas and threadfins to feed on crustaceans dislodged by the surf. Plain silvery when swimming, it can put on 7 vertical body bars when at rest. **Range:** Chesapeake Bay and Bahamas to Brazil, including the Gulf of Mexico. **Edibility:** good.

Reef croaker (caimuire) *Odontoscion dentex* To 1 foot. As its name implies, this croaker and the four *Equetus* genus drums (see following) are reef dwellers with a different life-style than that of other drums and croakers. The reef croaker may be seen in small aggregations hiding in reef crevices by day. It emerges at night to feed on crustaceans and small fishes. **Range:** Florida Keys to Bahia, Brazil. **Edibility:** fair.

High hat, striped drum (obispo) *Equetus acuminatus* To 9 inches. Juveniles of this species and other *Equetus* drums are incredible little creatures to see on the reef. All have extremely elongated dorsal, ventral and tailfins, and they resemble tiny, lovely oriental kites floating languidly in the blue tides. Adults and juveniles are often seen during the day in small groups hiding in or hovering near coral reefs, rock ledges, or rocky outcroppings in mixed sand and seagrass beds. At night they leave their hideaways and poke about the sand flats in search of food. Formerly known as *Equetus pulcher*, this fish is now the official "high hat." **Range:** South Carolina, Bermuda, Bahamas and Florida south through the Lesser Antilles. **Edibility:** poor.

ly it is to have sciaenids. Hawaii has not a single drum or croaker. One reason for the dependence of sciaenids on continental waters is their need for estuaries for breeding the young. A number of sciaenids have developed a completely freshwater existence.

Cubbyu (obispo) *Equetus umbrosus* To 9 inches. This drum is almost identical to the high hat, *Equetus acuminatus*, in all respects except for the blackish dorsal, caudal, anal and ventral fins. Some authorities still consider this fish to be simply a dark-tinged subspecies of *Equetus acuminatus*. The name-swapping between some of the *Equetus* genus drums is based on the recommendation of George C. Miller, and has been recognized by the American Fisheries Society. It is all quite confusing to the average fishwatcher and aquarium keeper, but the explanation is as follows: the fish known as the "striped drum" *Equetus pulcher*, is now recognized as the "high hat," *Equetus acuminatus*. The fish formerly known as the "cubbyu," *Equetus acuminatus*, still retains the common name "cubbyu," but the scientific name has changed to *Equetus umbrosus*. So far as is known, the cubbyu's life style and habitat are quite similar to the high hat. The cubbyu is reported to be "occasional" at Alligator Reef, Florida by Walter Starck, and is common off Florida's West Coast. **Range:** uncertain—see above. **Edibility:** poor.

☐ Unique among the drums and favorites of aquarists are the beautifully striped species of the genus *Equetus*, the high hat, cubbyu, striped drum and jackknife fishes. These lovely drums, unlike other sciaenids, are reef dwellers. They are secretive by day, and are typically found either solitary, in pairs or small groups, hiding under rock ledges or in reef crevices. They are completely at home on the reef, do not depend on estuarine waters to spawn, and consequently are found throughout the West Indies to Central and South America.

Spotted drum (obispo) *Equetus punctatus* To 11 inches. Originally thought to be extremely rare, this shy drum was observed by scientists in Tektite I and II Man-in-the-Sea Programs and by Starck and Davis to be very secretive, hiding deep in reef crevices by day, but emerging at night to forage boldly for crustaceans, polychaetes and gastropods. Similar to the jackknife fish, it is easily distinguished by the dark-colored and spotted dorsal and tail fins, and the multiple (rather than single) body bars. A very striking and impressive aquarium fish. **Range:** Florida, Bahamas through Greater Antilles. **Edibility:** poor.

Jackknife fish (obispo) *Equetus lanceolatus* To 9 inches. A beautiful animal, both on and under the reef and in the aquarium. The elongated first dorsal fin is even more impressive in juveniles, and the fin is used almost like an antenna by all the long-dorsal-finned *Equetus* genus drums. In the aquarium the spine is erected like a warrior's lance if the fish is startled, threatened or frightened, and at feeding times. It serves effectively as a deterrent to predators, since, with the fin erected, the little drum is very difficult to swallow. The Spanish name "obispo" (bishop) likens the long dorsal fin to the high pointed hat of a bishop. **Range:** Carolinas, Bermuda and Bahamas to the hump of Brazil. **Edibility:** poor.

Spot, goody, lafayette (chopa blanca) *Leiostomus xanthurus*
To 14 inches. Small, but one of the tastiest panfishes of the sea,
the popular spot feeds close inshore on crustaceans, worms and
mollusks. Abundant one year, scarce the next; anglers lower
bloodworms from anchored boats to catch the spot. Commercial
fishermen of Norfolk, Virginia and South Carolina land much of
the nearly 10 million pounds annual catch. **Range:** Cape Cod to
Florida and across the Gulf Coast to Texas. **Edibility:** excellent.

Atlantic croaker (roncador, corvina, blanca) *Micropogon undula-
tus* To 20 inches. From Cape Cod to Texas, anglers pursue the
croaker or "hardhead" bottom fishing over sandy bottoms, where
the fish probes with sensitive barbels for worms, crustaceans and
mollusks. Exceedingly abundant on the Gulf Coast. **Range:**
Massachusetts to Mexico. A closely related species, *M. furnieri*,
ranges through the West Indies to Venezuela. **Edibility:** good.

PORGIES, SEA BREAMS, CHUBS, SPADEFISHES

Spot porgy, silver porgy, spottail pinfish (San Pedra) *Diplodus holbrooki* To 1 foot. A sociable, active fish of the surf zone and near-shore reefs, the spot porgy swims peaceably in the company of chubs, mojarras, threadfins and croakers. **Range:** South Florida, Bahamas throughout Caribbean. **Edibility:** fair.

A familiar and pleasing sight to divers in Southern Florida, the Bahamas, and the Caribbean is the brilliant and sparkling spot porgy, also known as the spottail pinfish or silver porgy. Easily identified by the large round black spot on the tail, these silvery beauties may be seen singly or in schools of from 10 to 30 fishes, often in the company of chubs and sea breams. Porgies, of the family **Sparidae**, are related to the grunts, and they look somewhat like a cross between a round-headed snapper and a grunt. They are not often seen by divers, partly due to their extreme wariness. Many porgies are bottom dwellers and some range out to 250 ft. depths. Shellfish are a major part of their diet and they are equipped with powerful incisor and molar-like teeth to crush and grind shells. Though occasionally seen around rocks and coral reefs, they are not reef dwellers. If attacked, they rely on their speed and agility to outdistance pursuers, rather than hiding in reef crevices. In general, porgies are excellent food fishes.

☐ Chubs, of the family Kyphosidae, are also known as rudder-fishes because of their habit of following in the wake of ships. Bermuda chubs are especially fond of trailing ships, and have been known to follow them for hundreds of miles into the West Atlantic. Chubs are plant-feeding fishes that are often caught on hook and line. They are excellent game fishes that fight powerfully when hooked, but they are poor food fishes and are usually released when caught. They often school along with porgies, especially the spot porgy, which they superficially resemble.

Jolthead porgy (bajonado) *Calamus bajonado* To 2 feet. The largest of the porgies, the jolthead reportedly got its name from the way it "jolts" or shakes mollusks loose from rocks and pilings with its powerful jaws. A splendid table fish with firm, moist, white flesh. **Range:** Rhode Island south to Bermuda, Bahamas, Florida to Brazil, including the Gulf of Mexico. **Edibility:** excellent.

Saucereye porgy (pez de pluma) *Calamus calamus* To 16 inches. A very rapid color-changer, this fish can go to striped or blotched coloration in a twinkling. Young are found in seagrass beds; adults over the reefs. Has been taken from near-shore to 250 feet. **Range:** North Carolina, Bermuda, Bahamas and Florida to British Honduras, including the Gulf of Mexico. **Edibility:** good.

□ One of the most impressive sights in the underwater world is a large school of spadefishes. These magnificent fishes (family Ephippidae), reaching lengths of 3 feet, seem curious about divers, and have been known to circle the diver, literally walling him in by a silvery, moving cylinder of spadefishes. They have a vast range, from Massachusetts to Brazil. Recently introduced to Bermuda, they seem to be doing well there. They are virtually omnivorous, with a special craving for shellfish.

Red porgy (guerito) *Pagrus sedecim* To 20 inches. This is a deepwater porgy that is often taken along with red snappers on the snapper banks of Florida from Pensacola south. Numerous red porgies are also taken by commercial fishermen in bottom trawls fished off the coast of the southeastern United States. **Range:** New York to Argentina including the Gulf of Mexico, but not the West Indies. **Edibility:** good.

Sheepshead porgy (pez de pluma) *Calamus penna* To 18 inches. Ranges from near shore to 270 feet. A bottom fish, it may flash to a barred coloration when it is on or near the bottom. **Range:** Bahamas and Florida to Brazil, including the Gulf of Mexico. **Edibility:** good.

Grass porgy, shad porgy *Calamus arctifrons* To 10 inches. A small porgy, rather common in shallow water seagrass patches on both coasts of Florida and in the eastern Gulf from Louisiana to Florida. Though small, it is valued as a good panfish. **Range:** see above. **Edibility:** good.

Sheepshead, convict fish (sargo) *Archosargus probatocephalus* To 3 feet. A popular game and food fish, especially in Florida. Like most of the porgies, the sheepshead is a very suspicious, wary quarry, fond of lurking in holes and crevices. They feed on mollusks, crabs and barnacles which they noisily scrape off of rocks and pilings with their strong incisor teeth. **Range:** apparently restricted to continental coastlines, *A. probatocephalus* occurs from Nova Scotia to Florida and through the Gulf of Mexico to Yucatan, and a similar subspecies, *A. aries* occurs from British Honduras to Brazil. **Edibility:** excellent.

Pinfish, sailor's choice, pigfish, bream (chopa spina, sargo) *Lagodon rhomboides* To 14 inches. Ranging from Cape Cod south to Florida and throughout the Gulf of Mexico to Yucatan, this brilliant active little fish is extremely abundant, especially in the southern part of its range. Shore fishermen regularly take home strings of pinfish, and find them to be excellent eating. **Range:** see above. **Edibility:** good.

Sea bream (chopa amarilla, salema) *Archosargus rhomboidalis* To 13 inches. This handsome porgy and the pinfish are quite similar shallow-water fishes, and are often confused by Florida fishermen. They may be separated by noting the deeper body of the sea bream, and the blackish spot, larger than the eye, behind the gill cover. Formerly known as *A. unimaculatus.* **Range:** Florida through the West Indies to Brazil, including the Gulf of Mexico. **Edibility:** good.

Scup *Stenotomus chrysops* To 18 inches. Abundant on the east coast of the U.S., this popular and excellent table fish is called scup in New England, porgy in New York, maiden, fair maid and ironsides in Chesapeake Bay, and porgy again in the Carolinas. Anglers bait the hook with shellfish, anchor over sandy bottoms, and reel in scup by the score. A very similar scup, *S. caprinus*, replaces *S. chrysops* in the Gulf of Mexico. **Range:** *S. chrysops*, Nova Scotia to Florida; *S. caprinus*, South Carolina south through the Gulf of Mexico. **Edibility:** good.

Spadefish (chirivita chiva) *Chaetodipterus faber* To 3 feet. Found around reefs, piers, wrecks and bridges, and common around offshore oil platforms in the Gulf of Mexico. Large schools of up to 500 spadefishes are occasionally seen off Bimini. Tiny all-black juveniles drift motionless near shore, mimicking leaves, mangrove pods and floating trash, as does the tripletail. **Range:** New England, Bermuda (introduced), Bahamas, Florida to southeastern Brazil, including the Gulf of Mexico. **Edibility:** good.

65

Bermuda chub (chopa, morocoto) *Kyphosus sectatrix* To 30 inches. These fishes appear as silvery or steel gray to the diver on the reef. On close inspection, the yellow markings and fine striping become visible. Some fishes in a small school will flash to a white-spotted coloration on occasion, especially when chasing other fishes. **Range:** both sides of the Atlantic; in the West Atlantic from New England to Bermuda, the Bahamas and Florida to Brazil. **Edibility:** variable—sometimes quite good; other times very poor.

Yellow chub (chopa) *Kyphosus incisor* To 26½ inches. Very like the Bermuda chub, but the yellow stripes on this fish are more pronounced, as are the yellow head markings. Both the yellow and Bermuda chubs are plant feeders, usually found over rocky bottoms, seagrass beds and coral reefs. Both are powerful fighters when hooked. **Range:** both sides of the Atlantic; in the West Atlantic from New England, the Bahamas and Florida to Brazil. **Edibility:** variable—sometimes quite good; other times very poor.

ANGELFISHES

JUVENILE

INTERMEDIATE

ADULT

French angelfish (chirivita, cachama negra) *Pomacanthus paru*
To 1¼ feet. The French angel is a splendid fish to see on the reef.
Juveniles are occasionally seen stationed at a coral head, picking
and cleaning parasites from larger fishes. Many inch-long French
juveniles have bright blue borders on their ventral fins and a blue
spot on the anal fin. French angels may be distinguished from
gray angels by their more rounded tails (especially in the young).
The adult french angel is a much darker fish than the gray, has
golden edges to the body scales, and a yellow bar at the base of
the pectoral fin. **Range:** both sides of the Atlantic. In the
Western Atlantic, from the Bahamas, Florida and the Gulf of
Mexico to southeastern Brazil. **Edibility:** poor.

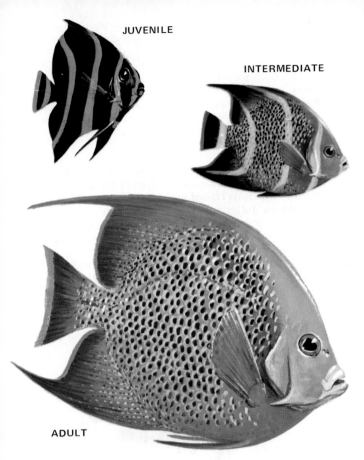

JUVENILE

INTERMEDIATE

ADULT

Gray angelfish, black angelfish (chirivita, cachama blanca) *Pomacanthus arcuatus* To 2 feet. This impressive fish appears to be the hardiest of the West Atlantic angelfishes—stragglers have been taken as far north as New York. The yellow pectoral fins and the square-cut tail separate it from the French angel, which it superficially resembles. Juveniles are beautifully colored with yellow stripes on a black body. French and gray angelfish juveniles are so alike that it is extremely difficult to distinguish between them. Probably the best identifier is the tail fin—the French angel juvenile has a more rounded tail fin, while that of the young gray angel is usually more truncate and rectangular. **Range:** New England to southeastern Brazil, including the Gulf of Mexico. **Edibility:** poor.

The most vividly beautiful fishes in the West Atlantic, without doubt, are the dazzling angelfishes. The black and gold brilliance of the rock beauty, the regal splendor of the queen and blue angels, the French angel with its jet-black body speckled with gold, and the more subdued beauty of the gray angel bring joy to the fishwatcher wherever they are seen. Not content with one brilliant color phase, each of these fishes has juvenile and intermediate color stages that rival the adult, as shown on these pages.

☐ Closely related to the butterflyfishes, the angelfishes (family Pomacanthidae) are so like the butterflies that they are frequently classed in the same family. They differ from the butterflies in having a strong, sharp spine at the lower edge of each gill plate. Perhaps because of this extra weapon, which they use to good effect in battle, angelfishes seem a bit more aggressive than the more timid and retiring butterflies. Angelfishes are frequently seen in pairs, and they are very sensitive about their territory. They will defend it stoutly against all comers.

Cherubfish, pygmy angelfish *Centropyge argi* To 2¾ inches. This pygmy member of the angelfish family was first described in 1951 from a single Bermudan specimen taken in 1908. In 1952 another was found in the stomach of a snapper off Yucatan. No more were found until 1959, when members of the Miami Seaquarium staff netted a number of cherubfishes off Bimini. Since then alert divers have encountered numerous others in the Bahamas and elsewhere. Walter Starck reports it as "occasional" at Alligator Reef, Florida. They appear to be more common in water over 100 feet in depth. **Range:** Bermuda, Bahamas, south Florida, West Indies, Gulf of Mexico. **Edibility:** poor.

☐ West Atlantic angelfish species vary in size from the dainty cherubfish reaching 2¾ inches to the magnificent gray angelfish which grows to 2 feet. Most angels feed heavily on invertebrates, principally sponges and tunicates, but algae is also an important part of their diet. Juvenile angelfishes have feeding habits quite different from those of adults. Some juveniles have been seen stationed at coral reef "cleaning stations," where they pick parasites from larger fishes who come for the service. Angelfishes are not numerous in the West Atlantic, and they can be (and have been) completely eliminated in certain easily accessible diving locales. Their curiosity and boldness makes them easy targets for thoughtless spearfishermen and fish collectors.

Rock beauty (vaqueta de dos colores, cachama medio luto) *Holacanthus tricolor* To 1 foot. Adults are conspicuous and unmistakable and a delight to see. Although they are not abundant anywhere, they are fairly common in the West Indies. Bright orange-yellow juveniles might be confused with the 3-spot damselfish (page 78) except the damsel has 3 spots (one on the tail) instead of 2. **Range:** Florida to southeastern Brazil; stragglers reach Georgia and Bermuda. **Edibility:** poor.

JUVENILE

ADULT

Queen angelfish (isabelita, cachama de piedra) *Holacanthus ciliaris* To 1½ feet. This gaudy, magnificent animal can be almost inconspicuous in its natural habitat among the blue and yellow-dappled sea whips, sea fans and corals. Can easily be confused with the blue angelfish, but adult blues lack the regal corona spotted with blue over the eye. Queens also have all-yellow tails and pectoral fins while blue angels have blue pectoral and tail fins with only the outer edges yellow. **Range:** Bermuda and Bahamas to Brazil, including the Gulf of Mexico. **Edibility:** poor.

Juvenile queen and **blue angels** are quite difficult to distinguish. They all have yellow pectorals and yellow tails, and whitish-blue stripes on the sides which vary greatly with growth. Usually, the second bold blue bar on the body of the young queen angel is curved, while on the young blue angel it is more straight as shown. Under about 2 inches, both queen and blue angel juveniles have the basic pattern of 3 light blue body bars on a dark body. As the fish grows, the bars first increase in number, then gradually disappear.

JUVENILE

ADULT

Blue angelfish *Holacanthus bermudensis* To 1½ feet. This fish has a splendor of its own—a more subdued version of the queen angel. The queen and blue angelfishes apparently freely interbreed, resulting in hybrid forms which are intermediate in color. This led to much confusion in the description and naming of the blue angelfish. It was previously known as *H. isabelita*. The name *H. townsendi* is based on a hybrid specimen between the queen and blue angelfishes. **Range:** Rare in the Bahamas, but common in Bermuda, and Florida. Ranges through the West Indies and the Gulf of Mexico. **Edibility:** poor.

JUVENILE

ADULT

BUTTERFLYFISHES

Bank butterflyfish *Chaetodon aya* To 5 inches. A fairly rare deepwater butterflyfish distinctive for the high, strong dorsal and anal fin spines, long snout and bold oblique bars transversing its body. This fish seems to inhabit deep, offshore reefs and much colder water than most butterflyfishes. **Range:** Reported from North Carolina, Georgia, and taken in the Gulf of Mexico from hard offshore bottoms east of the Mississippi delta in five (rare) to 25 fathoms. Also a sighting reported in the "Flower Gardens" coral reef off the Galveston, Texas coast. **Edibility:** poor.

Much like a marine butterfly, the butterflyfish flashes in yellow and black-banded beauty around West Atlantic coral reefs. The foureye, spotfin and banded butterflies are quite common throughout the tropical Western Atlantic and the Gulf of Mexico. They prefer coral reefs, but can be found around almost any rock formation, singly or in pairs, rarely in schools. Many butterfly species characteristically pair off at an early age (2 to 3 inches in length). The pair seem almost inseparable, and follow each other around as though attached by a string. The two fishes rigorously patrol their territory, and will defend it fearlessly against aggressors—especially other butterflies. Since butterflies do not raise their young, it has been a source of debate as to why they pair off, apparently for life. Hans Fricke theorizes that this is a means of guarding against faulty cross-breeding between species, thus insuring the purity of the breed.

□ The chaetodonts are disc-shaped fishes with small mouths set with bristle-like teeth (chaeta = bristle, odont = tooth). Some, like the longsnout butterfly, have forcep-like snouts for picking small invertebrates from coral crevices. West Atlantic butterflies range in size from 3½-inch species like the longsnout butterfly to the spotfin butterfly, which reaches 8 inches.

□ Although seemingly fragile and defenseless against the numerous predators of the reef, butterflyfish are able to survive by their rapidity, agility and defensive shape and coloring. They rarely stray far from the sheltering reef, and their narrow bodies fit easily into cracks and holes in the coral. If cornered, they lower their heads and spread their dorsal and anal spines, presenting the attacker with a difficult, prickly meal to swallow. Further, as

JUVENILE

ADULT

Foureye butterflyfish (isabelita) *Chaetodon capistratus* To 6 inches. The most common butterflyfish in the West Atlantic. This fish occurs in large numbers in the Bahamas and is abundant throughout the Caribbean. Juveniles have two eye-spots, and indistinct vertical body stripes that fade as the fish matures. **Range:** New England south through the Lesser Antilles, including the Gulf of Mexico. **Edibility:** poor.

74

Spotfin butterflyfish (isabelita) *Chaetodon ocellatus* To 8 inches. Easily identified by the small black dot on the outer edge of the soft dorsal fin, and the larger dusky spot on the inner edge of the soft dorsal fin. This butterfly undergoes a surprising change of color at night when all chaetodonts enter into a state of torpor. Broad, dusky dark bands appear on the body, and the large, pale spot on the soft dorsal becomes dark black. **Range:** New England south to Brazil, including the Gulf of Mexico. **Edibility:** poor.

JUVENILE

ADULT

Longsnout butterflyfish *Prognathodes aculeatus* To 3½ inches. Another deepwater butterflyfish, the longsnout is said to be the most common butterflyfish at depths over 100 feet. Nevertheless it has been sighted in the shallows (once in 3 feet of water) in such Caribbean locales as the Virgin Islands, Leeward Islands and Curacao. Its long snout enables it to pick invertebrates from coral crevices. Also feeds on the tubefeet of sea urchins, the tentacles of tubeworms, and various small crustaceans. **Range:** Florida and the Bahamas south through the Lesser Antilles, including the Gulf of Mexico. **Edibility:** poor.

shown in these illustrations, all West Atlantic butterflies possess a dark stripe or patch passing through and concealing their eyes. Some also have a false eye spot or "ocellus" located near the tail. Current theory holds that this false eye spot is designed to fool predators. The false eye spot is usually larger than the real eye, thus confusing the attacker as to the size of its prey, and the location of the head of the butterfly. Thus when the attacker lunges at the wrong end, the wily butterfly makes its escape to a nearby crevice.

Banded butterflyfish (isabelita) *Chaetodon striatus* To 6 inches. Strikingly banded in black at all stages. The young are especially so and make attractive aquarium inhabitants. Next to the four-eye butterfly, this is the commonest of West Atlantic butterfly-fishes. **Range:** Both sides of the Atlantic; in the West Atlantic from New Jersey to southeastern Brazil, including the Gulf of Mexico. **Edibility:** poor.

Reef butterflyfish (isabelita) *Chaetodon sedentarius* To 6 inches. This fish is fond of deeper water, thus it is rarely seen by divers. Walter A. Starck reports it is common at Alligator Reef, in the Florida Keys. Juveniles are almost identical to adults, except for a single small spot on the soft dorsal surrounded by a white ring. **Range:** Bermuda (rare) and the Bahamas; North Carolina to southern Florida, and the eastern Gulf of Mexico and the Caribbean. **Edibility:** poor.

DAMSELFISHES

ADULT

JUVENILE

Yellowtail damselfish (morocota) *Microspathodon chrysurus* To 6 inches. Both adults and juveniles of this species are truly splendid animals, unmistakable with their bright blue or white spots set like rhinestones across their bodies. Adults seem capable of paling their body color from black or dark blue to brown, russet or violet. A common fish on coral reefs. The young are often seen among the blades of yellow stinging coral (*Millepora*). Feeds on algae and organic detritus, coral polyps and other invertebrate animals. Juveniles have been seen picking at the bodies of larger fishes in search of parasites. **Range:** Bermuda, the Bahamas and Florida to northern coast of South America, including the Gulf of Mexico. **Edibility:** poor.

Occasionally divers are ferociously attacked by a dusky little 4-inch fish that dashes from its coral cranny and insistently rushes the intruder, sometimes nipping lightly at the diver's arms, legs or fins. This tiny reef marauder is the damselfish, one of the most courageous and pugnacious residents of the coral reef. Damsels will fearlessly attack large barracuda, jacks, parrotfishes or anything that threatens their coral home. The pomacentrids, or damsel-fishes, are small, tropical fishes distinguishable from most other marine species in having only one nostril on each side of the snout (instead of the usual two). They range in size from 2½ to 10 inches, and inhabit inshore reefs and tidepools over depths from 5 to 50 feet. Some range out to 180 foot and greater depths.

☐ Most pomacentrids spawn on the bottom, and unusual mating behavior has been reported among some species. The male fish sets up a strongly defended territory on a section of rock, and begins a series of invitations to pass-ing females indicating that he is ready to spawn. When an egg-bearing female sees him making his looping mo-tions over his territory and accepts his invitation, she is led to the cleared area. Some species of male damsels have been heard to emit a distinct churring sound—brrrrr—during spawning. It is deduced that this sound is an im-

ADULT

JUVENILE

Threespot damselfish *Pomacentrus planifrons* To 4½ inches. Though tiny, this fish is one of the most consistently aggressive animals in the world. It will fearlessly attack large jacks, group-ers, barracuda, crabs, even divers and TV cameras which venture near its territory. Yellow juveniles are easy to identify, with their bright yellow jackets and three-spot markings. They are likely to be confused only with the juvenile rock beauty (see page 70). Adult threespots are dusky and dark, and quite similar to numer-ous other adult damsels, including the dusky, beaugregory and cocoa damsels. The fairly deep, rounded body and yellowish tinge are good identification aids for the adult threespot. **Range:** Ber-muda, Bahamas and southern Florida south through the Carib-bean. **Edibility:** poor.

portant component of mating, without which the female would not lay eggs. Once she has deposited all her eggs, the male fertilizes them with his spawn; the female is chased from the nest, and the male continues his looping mating signals. When several females have deposited their eggs he takes total responsibility, fanning the eggs with his fins to oxygenate them, and guarding them ferociously against all predators. Large fishes and even skindivers have been chased and routed by worried male damsels. His vigil ends when the eggs hatch and the tiny damsels are left to fend for themselves on the vast, teeming reef.

ADULT

JUVENILE

Dusky damselfish (leopoldito) *Pomacentrus fuscus* To 6 inches. Adults are fond of mixed sand and rocky tidepool areas. I have found areas of tumbled rocks close to shore where virtually every large rock was closely guarded by a pugnacious little dusky damsel. Young are brilliant little fishes as shown, bright blue with the distinctive orange wash running across the nape and into the dorsal fin. It is often difficult to distinguish an adult dusky damsel from the very similar adult cocoa, beaugregory or threespot, but if the fish is almost entirely dusky bluish-blackish-brown with little hint of yellow, it is probably a dusky damsel. Note the small black spot at the upper edge of the pectoral base. **Range:** Bermuda, Bahamas and Florida through the Caribbean, including the Gulf of Mexico. **Edibility:** poor.

79

Beaugregory *Pomacentrus leucostictus* To 4 inches. The young beaugregory is a lovely, ubiquitous animal, common in calm, shallow tidepools, rock, sand and seagrass bottoms of a few inches in depth out to coral reefs over 20 feet deep. As they grow, they become uniformly dusky, much like the other dusky damsels, except for the tail, which remains relatively pale. They retain the blue spots on the nape and dorsal and the dark spot on the soft dorsal well into adulthood. As they age, these features disappear completely. One aid to identification is the torpedo shape of the beaugregory—it is the most shallow bodied fish of the genus. It has no spot on the tail base. **Range:** Maine to Bermuda, the Bahamas, Florida and the Gulf of Mexico and throughout the Caribbean to the hump of Brazil. **Edibility:** poor.

ADULT

JUVENILE

JUVENILE

ADULT

Cocoa damselfish *Pomacentrus variabilis* To 4¼ inches. One of the non-aggressive damsels, the cocoa swims peaceably about its home range, picking and plucking at the coral or bottom. The cocoa damsel is not as common as the previous three fishes, but neither is it a rare fish. The problem of trying to distinguish between adults and juveniles of the *Pomacentrus* genus damsels becomes evident when comparing the cocoa damsel with the last three species. They all have striking similarities, and it takes a sharp eye underwater to separate them. The cocoa damsel is not deep-bodied like the threespot damsel, and there is on most fishes (not all) a pronounced spot on the tail base of both young and adults. It might be confused with the dusky damsel, but the adult cocoa is more suffused with yellow than the dusky adult. **Range:** Bahamas and Florida to Brazil, including the Gulf of Mexico. **Edibility:** poor.

Bicolor damselfish *Pomacentrus partitus* To 4 inches. Fairly common on isolated patch reefs at depths of from 25 to 75 feet, and can be seen occasionally in shallow water. One was taken from a depth of over 1200 feet off Puerto Rico. Male bicolors guard egg clusters anchored to the substrate by filaments, and they can be quite pugnacious when on guard. **Range:** Bahamas and Florida and throughout the Caribbean. **Edibility:** poor.

Honey gregory, honey damselfish *Pomacentrus mellis* To 2½ inches. A rare and striking fish that seems to retain the same coloration in all phases of growth. Because of its pattern of violet lines and dots, the honey damsel might be mistaken for the cocoa or beaugregory juveniles, but both of these fishes possess a blue wash over nape and dorsal that the honey gregory lacks. No spot at base of tail fin. One of the smallest of the damsels. **Range:** Bahamas and Florida through the West Indies to Venezuela. **Edibility:** poor.

Blue chromis *Chromis cyaneus* To 5 inches. Look for this splendid fish in the blue water above the deep outer reefs and patch reefs. Mixed with clouds of blue chromis you will often find brown chromis and the wrasse that mimics the blue chromis, the creole wrasse (see page 96). These fishes feed on the zooplankton floating in the water column, and they can be seen picking copepods, one by one, from the passing water mass. **Range:** Bermuda, Bahamas, and Florida south through the Caribbean. **Edibility:** poor.

Brown chromis, yellow-edge chromis *Chromis multilineatus* To 6 inches. Very like the blue chromis in all respects save color, and the two fishes often swim together in large aggregations over reefs, picking plankton (mostly copepods) from the water mass. Note the dark blotch at the base of the pectoral fin, and the white spot behind the soft dorsal fin. *Chromis marginatus* is a synonym. **Range:** Bermuda, Bahamas and Florida south through the Lesser Antilles. **Edibility:** poor.

Yellowtail reeffish *Chromis enchrysurus* To about 4 inches. A deep-bodied fish quite similar in shape to the sunshine fish (see following), but with 2 violet stripes near the eye and a distinctive yellow tail. Fairly rare in shallow water, but quite common at 90 to 130 foot depths. **Range:** Both coasts of Florida; in the Gulf of Mexico it prefers deepwater reefs and hard bottoms from Pensacola, Florida south. **Edibility:** poor.

Sunshine fish, olive damselfish *Chromis insolatus* To 4 inches. The only green damsel in the West Atlantic, the juvenile sunshine fish is a brilliant animal, lime green or bright yellow above, dull olive below. As the fish matures, this bicolor pattern fades, and the damsel becomes olivaceous overall. A deepwater fish, it ranges from 50 to 160 feet off the Florida Keys, where Walter Starck finds it in abundance. In the Bahamas it has been taken at depths from 35 to 180 feet. Tends to stay close to the bottom, feeding on plankton. Often swims with the purple reeffish. **Range:** Bermuda and the Carolinas, Bahamas and Florida, south through the Lesser Antilles. **Edibility:** poor.

Purple reeffish *Chromis scotti* To 4 inches. Another deepwater damsel closely related to the sunshine fish. The purple reeffish is iridescent blue as a juvenile, purple-blue or dull blue as an adult. The deepwater chromis damsels have rounded, short, stubby bodies and only slightly-forked caudal fins that suits their bottom-dwelling existence. The high water chromis damsels (blue and brown chromis) on the other hand have more slender, streamlined bodies and deeply forked tails that enable them to maneuver rapidly in the shifting water mass high over the patch reefs. **Range:** reported from Bermuda, Florida and the eastern Gulf of Mexico from Pensacola south. **Edibility:** poor.

Night sergeant *Abudefduf taurus* To 10 inches. If you dive off any rocky inshore area such as a rock jetty or pier, you may find a few schools of night sergeants, peering cautiously out from their grottos. They prefer turbulent water, the shallower the better—I have found quite large night sergeants in as little as 2 feet of water. They are wary and evasive and since they are primarily herbivorous, they rarely take a fisherman's hook. **Range:** Florida, Bahamas and the Gulf of Mexico south to the Central American coast. **Edibility:** fair.

Sergeant major (petaca) *Abudefduf saxatilis* To 7 inches. The familiar sergeant major is found almost everywhere—over all kinds of bottoms from coral to sand to sea grass beds to rocky tide pools and dock pilings—eating with the most catholic of tastes— from anemones and tunicates to zooplankton, small fishes, algae and fisherman's bait. When guarding its egg patch from voracious wrasses, the adult male becomes dark bluish in color—so blue that at times the vertical body bars are almost obscured. **Range:** New England to Uruguay, including the Gulf of Mexico. **Edibility:** fair, but usually too small to warrant the effort.

SEE MAPS OF WEST ATLANTIC—
Pages 201-204

SEE TIPS FOR FISHWATCHERS—
Page 200

WRASSES

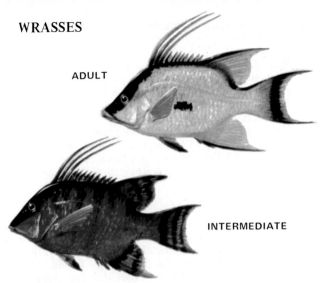

ADULT

INTERMEDIATE

Hogfish (el capitan, peje perro, pargo gallo) *Lachnolaimus maximus* To 3 feet. Unmistakable at all growth stages. Capable of various color changes from pale to mottled to banded, and from light grey to brick red. Aptly named, the hogfish is well-designed for rooting for food with its long snout. Large individuals have been observed rooting deep 6 to 9 inch holes in sand flats in search of mollusks, crabs and crustaceans. A popular food fish. Large 20 to 25 pound hogfish are now quite rare in some areas, owing to predation by spearfishermen. **Range:** North Carolina and Bermuda to Venezuela, including the Gulf of Mexico. **Edibility:** excellent.

If you see a small, gaudy, cigar-shaped fish pushing itself busily about the reef with its pectoral fins, you are watching a member of the wrasse (Labridae) family. West Atlantic wrasses occupy a variety of habitats. The blackear wrasse and the little green dwarf wrasse like sea grass beds where they hide easily in the blades of turtle grass. Razorfishes prefer sandy bottom or sea grass areas where they can dive quickly for cover. The creole wrasse swims with its look-alike, the blue chromis, high above the deeper patch reefs. Hogfishes (*L. maximus*) roam across open bottoms and sand flats where they feed on sea urchins and root happily for mollusks, crustaceans and worms. Most of the smaller cigar-shaped wrasses prefer the coral reefs and fan or sea-whip covered rocky flats.

Two exceptions are the bluehead and the slippery dick, which seem to move easily in virtually all habitats.

□ Many wrasses have the curious habit of burying themselves in the sand at night, and aquarium watchers are frequently surprised to find that a tank filled with wrasses by day will be completely barren at night—they are all tucked away sleeping in the bottom gravel. Closely related to the parrotfishes, the wrasses have many characteristics in common with the parrots. Many West Atlantic wrasses spin themselves a gelatinous cocoon "nightgown" for protection while sleeping at night, as do certain parrotfishes.

□ The colors of the labrids are astonishing in their beauty and variety. They glisten with gem-like spots, flecks, blotches, stripes and bars. Like the parrotfishes, the wrasses almost defy classification due to the startling color changes that occur as the fish mature. To add to the confusion, sex-related changes occur that can change a female to a male, and possibly a male to a female.

Spanish hogfish (loro gallo) *Bodianus rufus* To 2 feet. Not abundant anywhere, but not uncommon over reefs of 10 to 100 foot depths. Lovely jewel-like juveniles (quite similar in coloration to the fairy basslet, page 17) are occasionally seen working their cleaning stations, picking parasites from large jacks, groupers, and other predators. **Range:** Bermuda, Bahamas and Florida to Brazil, including the Gulf of Mexico. **Edibility:** good.

☐ Certain young juvenile wrasses become sexually mature as small as 1½ inches, and mate in groups. Group mating usually begins with upward spawning rushes by an egg-laden female. She is followed by numerous young males, all of whom assist in fertilizing eggs. A certain number of the males, and apparently some sex-reversed females, become terminal-phase supermales, emerging in brilliant hues of blue, green, red or yellow, and sporting flowing, lyre-like tails. These supermales tend to mate and spawn individually with one or more females. Dominant supermale wrasses of some species set up "harems" on the reef of from 4 to 10 females and actively mate with all members of the harem. If the supermale dies or is dispatched by a predator, the largest female in the harem changes into a supermale, and assumes the dominance and mating duties of the harem. On the larger reefs, the bluehead wrasse has a mating system whereby several dozen large supermales set up spawning territories in a restricted area of the reef. Each guards his area strongly against younger male wrasses. Each day near midday, females come to this area and select the largest and most brightly colored supermale for mating. Large supermales often spawn more than 40 times a day, and in high population areas, 100 times a day is not unusual. Small wonder that bluehead wrasses are so numerous.

Spotfin or Cuban hogfish *Bodianus pulchellus* To 9 inches. Quite similar in many respects to the Spanish hogfish, except for the coloration. Juveniles are cleaner fishes, like the Spanish hogfish. Up to 2 inches in length, young are all yellow with part-black dorsal fins. Rare in less than 50 feet of water and has been taken at 360 foot depths. **Range:** South Carolina, Bahamas, and Florida to Lesser Antilles. **Edibility:** poor.

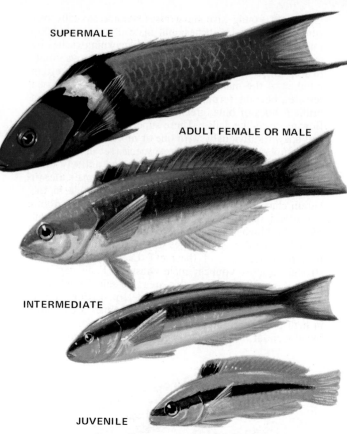

SUPERMALE

ADULT FEMALE OR MALE

INTERMEDIATE

JUVENILE

Bluehead *Thalassoma bifasciatum* To 6 inches. One of the most successful fish in the tropical West Atlantic, representatives of this species seem to be everywhere. Their brilliant yellow bodies dart in and out of coral reefs, rocky flats, reef sand and sea grass habitats. The name "bluehead" is a misnomer, since only the terminal phase male, constituting about 4% of the population, has a blue head. Adult females, adult males and juveniles are yellow-jacketed with a midlateral stripe or bar, as illustrated. In seconds these wrasses can flash from a broad midlateral stripe to a row of squarish blotches or bars, possibly to match their background. Yellow individuals have been seen to pick parasites from other fishes, and a recent observer found a large male bluehead cleaning another fish. **Range:** both sides of the Atlantic; in the West Atlantic, from Bermuda, Bahamas and Florida to Curacao, including the Gulf of Mexico. **Edibility:** poor.

☐ In size, West Atlantic wrasses vary from small species that attain a maximum length of 3 inches up to bull males of other species that reach 3 feet in length. Their flesh is generally soft and pasty, unattractive as food—with two exceptions. The hogfish, which grows to 3 feet, and the Spanish hogfish, reaching 2 feet, are considered excellent eating and are prize catches for fishermen.

☐ In the tropical West Atlantic the brilliant little juvenile Spanish and spotfin hogfish wrasses turn their home base coral heads into cleaning stations, and larger fishes come and often wait in line to be cleaned. Bluehead wrasses, juveniles and adults, have also been seen picking parasites off other fishes. It is an incredible sight to see these tiny wrasses fluttering about the fins, gills, and even into the mouths of huge jacks and groupers, predators that could easily dispatch them with a single gulp. Other fishes and

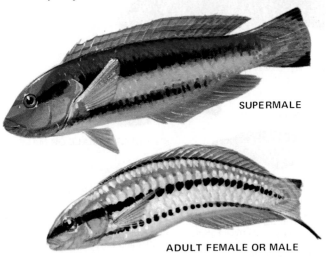

SUPERMALE

ADULT FEMALE OR MALE

Slippery dick (loro verde) *Halichoeres bivittatus* To 9 inches. One of the most abundant species of the genus, occurring in such diverse habitats as coral reef, sea-whip covered rocky flats, shallow reef and reef-sand areas. They feed mainly on crabs, sea urchins and mollusks. Easily distinguished by the two broad dark stripes on the sides of the body in virtually all phases. **Range:** North Carolina and Bermuda south to Brazil, including the Gulf of Mexico. **Edibility:** poor.

invertebrates that engage in symbiotic cleaning relationships with larger fishes include the cleaner goby and the sharknose goby (see page 167); and the scarlet lady and banded coral shrimps (see pages 189-190). One opportunistic fish, the wrasse blenny (see page 170), has gone to great lengths to mimic the bluehead cleaner wrasse. Thus it enjoys the same immunity from predation as the cleaner wrasse without having to work for it.

Yellowhead wrasse *Halichoeres garnoti* To 8 inches. Supermales, adult females and males and juveniles are quite unmistakable and distinct from other wrasses. Note the vividly blue-striped juvenile. A common inshore wrasse, but has been taken from 160 foot depths. **Range:** Bermuda, Bahamas and Florida to southeastern Brazil. **Edibility:** poor.

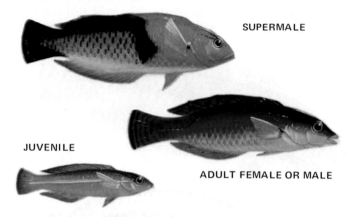

SUPERMALE

JUVENILE

ADULT FEMALE OR MALE

Rainbow wrasse, painted wrasse *Halichoeres caudalis* To 7 inches. This deep-dwelling wrasse is rarely seen by divers due to its preference for 90 to 240 foot depths. Note the black "ear" similar to the blackear wrasse. In the Gulf of Mexico it has been taken over deep reefs from Pensacola south and from the central Texas coast. **Range:** Florida, Greater Antilles and the Gulf of Mexico. **Edibility:** poor.

Clown wrasse *Halichoeres maculipinna* To 6½ inches. Both adult males and females and the splendid supermale are brilliantly painted in circus colors. A handsome fish to see on the reef, and voracious clown wrasses are common in many areas of the tropical West Atlantic. **Range:** North Carolina and Bermuda, Bahamas, and Florida to Brazil. **Edibility:** poor.

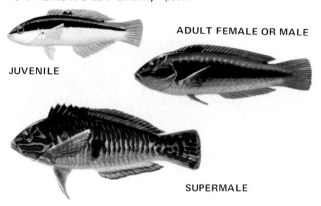

ADULT FEMALE OR MALE

JUVENILE

SUPERMALE

Blackear wrasse *Halichoeres poeyi* To 8 inches. Look for this wrasse in seagrass beds where it blends in perfectly with the blades of turtle grass. The black "ear" spot behind the eye is distinctive at all stages. Shown is the supermale and the yellow juvenile. Adult females and males appear very like the supermale, except they lack the red markings on the tail and have more subdued red spots and markings on the green body. **Range:** Bahamas and Florida to Brazil. **Edibility:** poor.

JUVENILE

SUPERMALE

92

JUVENILE

SUPERMALE

Puddingwife *Halichoeres radiatus* To 20 inches. The big super-male is unmistakable with its blue-green spots, stripes and worm-like scrawls. Smaller adult females, males and juveniles are almost totally different in coloration, but also unique. The 5 white spots just below the dorsal, broken by from one to two black blotches are distinctive, and present at all phases except the fully-grown supermale. **Range:** North Carolina, Bermuda, Bahamas, and Florida to Brazil. **Edibility:** poor.

Painted wrasse *Halichoeres pictus* To 6 inches. The painted wrasse is a coral reef species that stays well off the bottom, often swimming with bluehead and clown wrasses. The supermale is unmistakable. Younger males and females have two light brown stripes from nose to tail. Tiny juveniles are pale with a single lateral dark stripe. **Range:** Bahamas and Florida to the Lesser Antilles. **Edibility:** poor.

ADULT FEMALE OR MALE

SUPERMALE

93

Yellowcheek wrasse, yellowback wrasse *Halichoeres cyanocephalus* To 6 inches. An attractive yellow and blue striped wrasse not often seen by divers due to its preference for the deeper reefs. It was recently discovered (1965) off the American coast. Walter Starck reports that it is "frequent" at Alligator Reef, Florida. **Range:** uncertain. **Edibility:** poor.

Rosy or straighttail razorfish *Hemipteronotus martinicensis* To 6 inches. Most razorfishes possess compressed, razorlike heads, shaped almost like the prow of a ship. Since they burrow constantly into the gritty reef sand and gravel, a narrow forehead is a distinct asset. Shown is the adult male. Females are pale with a rosy stripe from eye to tail. **Range:** Bahamas to Venezuela, and west to Yucatan. **Edibility:** poor.

Green razorfish *Hemipteronotus splendens* To 4½ inches. If while diving you see a large-headed fish dive straight for the sand and disappear, that will be a razorfish. Longley at Tortugas found that green razorfishes always return to the same hiding place in the sand. They do not build nests, however, like the pearly razorfish. The adult male fish is shown. **Range:** Bermuda, Bahamas and Florida to Brazil. **Edibility:** poor.

Pearly razorfish *Hemipteronotus novacula* To 15 inches. Much like the sand tilefish, this fish burrows into the sand and builds a nest of coral fragments to which it returns if threatened by a predator. Also very adept at diving into the sand if alarmed. **Range:** the Carolinas, Bahamas and Florida to Brazil, including the Gulf of Mexico. **Edibility:** poor.

Cunner *Tautogolabrus adspersus* To 15 inches. The cunner is closely related to the tautog and these two fishes often swim together over much the same range. It is the northernmost of all the West Atlantic wrasses, ranging from Newfoundland to Chesapeake Bay. Young display blotches and dark bars. **Range:** see above. **Edibility:** good.

Tautog, blackfish, oysterfish *Tautoga onitis* To 3 feet. Ranging from Nova Scotia to South Carolina, the tautog is most abundant from Cape Cod to Delaware Bay. They are sluggish fishes, and divers often find them reclining on a rocky bottom or retreating reluctantly a few feet ahead. It is popular with anglers, and is taken to some extent in pots, traps and trawls. **Range:** see above. **Edibility:** good, but not extensively eaten.

Creole wrasse *Clepticus parrai* To 1 foot. This wrasse schools with and mimics the blue chromis damsels in open water around the deeper patch reefs. It can be distinguished from the damsel-fishes by its heavier body, broader tail and purple coloration. It also stubbornly swims with its pectoral fins in typical wrasse fashion. **Range:** North Carolina and Bermuda, the Bahamas and Florida south through the West Indies. **Edibility:** poor.

Dwarf wrasse *Doratonotus megalepis* To 3 inches. The smallest of the West Atlantic wrasses, this little fish is quite common over its range, yet rarely seen. It lives in shallow seagrass beds, and can change its coloration to exactly match its turtle grass background. **Range:** both sides of the Atlantic; in the West Atlantic from Bermuda, the Bahamas and Florida south through the Lesser Antilles. **Edibility:** poor.

PARROTFISHES

JUVENILE

ADULT FEMALE AND MALE

SUPERMALE

Queen parrotfish (vieja) *Scarus vetula* To 2 feet. So different are the male and female queen parrotfishes that earlier fish experts assumed that they were two different species and gave the name *Scarus gnathodus* to the female. The queen parrotfish has been seen to occur in "harems" of three or four females to one supermale, grazing together like cows and a bull. Known to envelop themselves in cocoons at night. For identification of the supermale, note the distinct markings on the nose, pectoral fins and tail, and the lunate tail. **Range:** Bermuda, Bahamas and Florida throughout the Caribbean to Venezuela. **Edibility:** poor.

If you dive off any shallow coral reef as the tide is coming in you are likely to encounter dozens of gaudy parrotfishes. They swarm in over the reef in blue-green, grey and rust-colored waves, grazing like guernsey cows through the coral. Many parrots are large, bulky fishes and they must wait for high tide to flood the close-packed coral reefs to give them room to maneuver and feed. They are single-minded, gentle creatures of habit, and they have their set patterns of travel. Occasionally I have come nose-to-nose with a large parrotfish in a narrow defile, and I had to back off respectfully to let it pass. They are not easily deterred from their feeding routes, and they seem to regard the curious diver with tolerance and some irritation for interrupting their non-stop, movable feast.

☐ Although closely related to the carnivorous wrasses, parrotfishes are herbivores of the Scaridae family. They are named for their gaudy colors and parrot-like beaks with which they bite away chunks of coral, leaving distinct beak-marks on the reef. In their constant quest for food, they are highly efficient recycling mechanisms. As they graze algae off the reefs, they turn coral and rock

ADULT FEMALE AND MALE

SUPERMALE

Rainbow parrotfish (guacamaya) *Scarus guacamaia* To 4 feet. One of the largest and most impressive of West Atlantic parrotfishes. Experiments at Bermuda indicate that this fish may use the sun for navigation. It traveled a considerable distance from its nocturnal home cave to feed by day and returned at evening in the same way, on a direct course to its cave. **Range:** Bermuda, Bahamas, and Florida south to Argentina. **Edibility:** poor.

98

into fine sand. They extract the algae by crushing the rock-hard coral with powerful plate-like pharyngeal teeth located in the back of the throat, then pass this stony rubble down an apparently cast-iron digestive tract. Due to their set patterns of travel and their almost constant defecation, they leave mounds and floors of fine sand and undigested coral rubble throughout the reef.

☐ Recent interest and knowledge of the scarids, speeded by the advent of scuba diving, has revealed that parrotfishes undergo dramatic color changes as they mature and, like the wrasses, sex changes as well. Most species mature through three different color phases, including juvenile, adult and "terminal phase" colorations. Male and female adults often share the same color pattern, but some males, as well as certain sex-reversed females, will

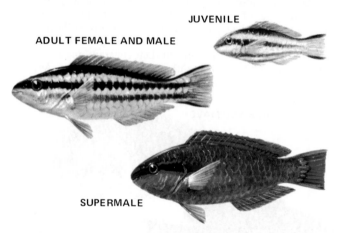

JUVENILE

ADULT FEMALE AND MALE

SUPERMALE

Princess parrotfish (pez loro) *Scarus taeniopterus* To 13 inches. The lavishly colored supermale seems to glow at times in red, blue and green neon. Much confusion has resulted from the close similarity in coloration between this fish and the mottlefin parrotfish, both supermales and females. Note the differences in the tail fins and the positions of the stripes around the eye. On the females, note the difference of the white striping on the head. On both females and juveniles, note the distinctive dark margins on the tail fin of the princess parrotfish. Known to produce cocoons at night. **Range:** Bermuda, Bahamas and Florida throughout Caribbean. Due to the confusion between the princess and mottlefin parrotfishes, the precise distribution of both species is uncertain. **Edibility:** poor.

99

mature into large terminal phase "supermales," sporting gaudy peacock colors and long, flowing tails. The reasons for these changes and the processes by which they occur are not well understood, but it is a subject of intense study in ichthyological circles. This startling new information has brought chaos to the inexact science of giving scientific names to the parrots. Of some 350 species of parrotfishes previously recorded throughout the world, a recent study reduced this number to 80 species, and many of these are in doubt. On-going studies continue to demonstrate that various fishes previously considered to be different species were actually male and female, or juvenile and adult specimens of the same fish species.

□ The considerable difference between male and female parrotfishes is clearly illustrated here by the queen, stoplight and redband parrots. In general, it is safe to say that most of the brilliant blue, green, red and lavishly striped and mottled parrots are adult terminal-phase males, while most of the dull grey, green red or brownish-colored

SUPERMALE

ADULT FEMALE AND MALE

Mottlefin or striped parrotfish (bullon) *Scarus croicensis* To 11 inches. Mottlefin is a particularly good name for the supermale of this species, since one of the key features that distinguishes it from the princess and queen parrotfish supermales is the blue mottling or marbling evident on all of the vertical fins. Also distinctive for the blue edges on the tail fin. Known to produce cocoons at night. **Range:** Bermuda, Bahamas, Florida south throughout the Caribbean, including the Gulf of Mexico. **Edibility:** poor.

parrots are females or immature males. Juvenile parrots 1½ to 4 inches long of most of the tropical West Atlantic species are colored a light grass green, grey or mottled green-brown, with various stripes, spots, bars and other markings across the body that differ according to the species.

□ Parrotfishes vary greatly in size. West Atlantic species range from the rosy parrot that attains an adult size of 4½ inches to the blue and rainbow parrots that reach 4 feet in length. It is a very impressive sight, when diving on the reef, to see a few 4 foot parrots browsing slowly among the coral heads. There have been reports of some Indo-Pacific parrots attaining lengths of 6 feet, and scattered claims of massive old bull males reaching 12 feet in length and 6 feet in depth. Even more strange, Jaques Yves Cousteau tells of seeing huge bumphead parrotfishes (*Bolbometapon muricatus*) charging at high speeds and smashing their curious, bumper-like heads into the reef to dislodge pieces of coral, which they would then munch contentedly in the manner of most parrots.

JUVENILE

ADULT FEMALE AND MALE

SUPERMALE

Blue parrotfish (loro azul, guacamaya) *Scarus coeruleus* To 4 feet. Both adult males and females are usually an even cerulean blue, but are capable of phasing to a mottled blue and black pattern to match the background. Large supermales develop the characteristic hump on the forehead. Beebe and Tee-Van report sighting a vast school of thousands of blue parrotfishes at 30 feet off Bermuda, all headed down and out toward open sea. **Range:** Virginia and Bermuda south to Brazil. **Edibility:** poor.

Another remarkable characteristic of certain parrots and a few wrasses is their habit of laboriously fabricating a mucous cocoon or "sleeping bag" around themselves before bedding down in the coral at night. Some species take 30 minutes to produce the cocoon at night, and another 30 minutes to break out of it in the morning. How and why the cocoon is made is a mystery. One theory postulates that the mucous cocoon serves to protect the sleeping fish from such night predators as moray eels, which depend on their keen sense of smell to locate their prey.

□ Tropical West Atlantic parrots are divided into two main genera—the genus *Sparisoma* and the genus *Scarus.* *Sparisoma* parrots have the 'beak' of the upper jaw en-

Midnight parrotfish, indigo parrotfish *Scarus coelestinus* To 30 inches. I spotted my first midnight parrotfish at Cozumel, Mexico and was so impressed that I followed it for 10 or 15 minutes while it munched algae off rocks and coral. A truly beautiful animal. Color is the same at all growth stages. **Range:** Bermuda, Bahamas and Florida to Brazil. **Edibility:** poor.

Emerald parrotfish *Nicholsina usta* To 1 foot. A wide-ranging parrotfish, found along the east coast of the U.S. from New Jersey to Florida, the Gulf of Mexico and the Greater Antilles to Brazil. Seems to prefer sea grass beds, but has been taken from close inshore to 240 foot depths. **Range:** see above. **Edibility:** poor.

Rosy parrotfish, slender, many-tooth or bluelip parrotfish *Cryptotomus roseus* To 4½ inches. This cigar-shaped little parrotfish is quite wrasse-like in shape and habits. Prefers grassy areas, tidal canals, turtle grass beds. Shown is the adult male. In the aquarium has been observed at night wrapped in a mucous cocoon and buried in the sand with only its head protruding. **Range:** Bermuda, Bahamas, and Florida to Brazil. **Edibility:** poor.

Redband parrotfish (pez loro) *Sparisoma aurofrenatum* To 11 inches. A much smaller fish than the stoplight, but has many similarities. The supermale can be distinguished from the stoplight supermale by the more squarecut tail, with black outer margins, the two black spots surrounded by yellow behind the eye, and the black spot at the base of the pectoral fin. The redband female and young are easily identified underwater by the white blotch or saddle just behind the dorsal fin. **Range:** Bermuda, Bahamas and Florida to Brazil. **Edibility:** poor.

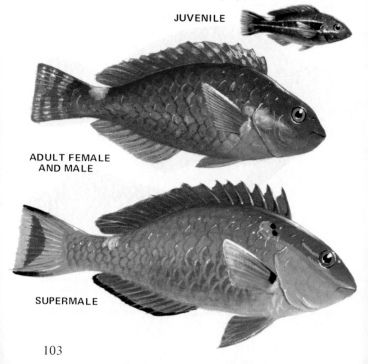

JUVENILE

ADULT FEMALE
AND MALE

SUPERMALE

closed by the beak of the lower jaw when the mouth is closed. This condition is reversed in the genus *Scarus*, where the upper 'beak' encloses the lower. Some of the *Scarus* parrots occasionally sleep in cocoon nightgowns (the rainbow, blue, princess and striped parrots), while others do not. *Sparisoma* parrots apparently do not spin cocoons. The rosy parrotfish of the genus *Cryptotomus* is smaller and more wrasse-like in shape and habits than any of the other parrots shown here. The rosy parrot not only spins a cocoon sleeping bag at night, but like the wrasses also buries itself in the sand, apparently for double protection.

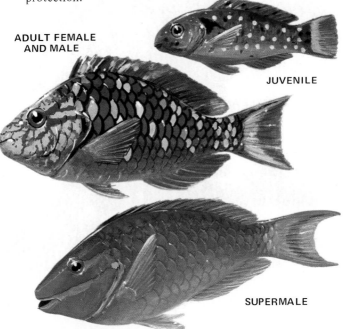

ADULT FEMALE AND MALE

JUVENILE

SUPERMALE

Stoplight parrotfish (macho—loro verde; hembra—loro colorado) *Sparisoma viride* To 21 inches. Supermales are distinguished from the similar redband parrot by their lunate, flowing tails and the distinctive gold spot at the upper corner of the gill cover. The harlequin-garbed red-bellied female and immature male are lovely animals to see on the reef. Even the tiny juvenile stoplight is a handsome spotted fish. **Range:** Bermuda, Bahamas and Florida to the hump of Brazil, including the Gulf of Mexico. **Edibility:** poor, but a market fish in Puerto Rico.

104

Redtail parrotfish (loro verde, cotoro verde) *Sparisoma chrysopterum* To 18 inches. This fish moves easily from coral reef to rocky areas to seagrass beds, and is a great color changer, adept at matching its background. Usually it is a very mottled gray-green fish and usually (but not always) with a red tail. Look for the distinct black spot at the pectoral fin base and the white saddle behind the dorsal fin on mature males and females, as well as on striped and spotted nondescript young. **Range:** Florida and the Bahamas to Brazil. **Edibility:** poor, but eaten in Puerto Rico.

ADULT FEMALE AND MALE

SUPERMALE

Bucktooth parrotfish (pez loro) *Sparisoma radians* To 7½ inches. Another expert color-changer, the sea-grass-dwelling bucktooth has an infinite variety of mottlings, patches, blotches and stripes to match any background in sea-grass, sand or rocky substrate. Shown is the mature male. Females and young males lack the bold black markings of the mature males, and have a light blue spot at the pectoral fin base (instead of black and a light blue margin on the gill cover. **Range:** Bermuda, Bahamas and Florida to Venezuela, including the Gulf of Mexico. **Edibility:** poor.

Yellowtail parrotfish (pez loro) *Sparisoma rubripinne* To 18 inches. The yellow-tailed females and young males are very common close inshore. Their nondescript, mottled coloration aids them in eluding predators by expertly matching their background. Large supermales were originally thought to be a separate species, *Sparisoma axillare*. **Range:** Massachusetts, Bermuda, Bahamas and Florida to Brazil. **Edibility:** poor.

ADULT FEMALE AND MALE

SUPERMALE

CARDINALFISHES

Bigtooth cardinalfish *Apogon affinis* To 4½ inches. At night this cardinalfish moves up to occupy the same plankton feeding area high in the water column vacated by the diurnal blue and brown chromis damselfishes. It is called "bigtooth" because of the large, distinct canines in its jaws. During the day it frequents dark caves, overhangs and hollow coral heads at depths of 50 feet or more, thus it is rarely seen by divers. **Range:** Bahamas and Florida Keys to Venezuela. **Edibility:** poor.

As dusk descends over the reef, and after all of the daylight-active fishes have retired to their reef holes and crevices for the night, there is a short period of calm and inactivity. One by one, like sentries on guard duty, the cardinalfishes appear. These large-eyed, nocturnal fishes are tiny, seldom over 5 inches in length. But they are so numerous and occupy such a variety of habitats that they are virtually the masters of the night reef. The bigtooth cardinalfishes rise from reef holes and bottom crevices high in the water column to occupy the same stations vacated by the chromis damselfishes. The conchfish, a tiny cardinal that hides during daylight hours in the mantle cavity of the queen conch, comes boldly out at night to forage across the reef bottom. The whitestar cardinalfish, a reef hole and cave dweller by day, moves very little at night, feeding quite near its daytime habitat. These minimasters of the night reef occupy the same stations vacated by various fishes active only during the day. All of them feed on zooplankton in the tides that sweep the reef, and their shift-like day-night activity assures that each fish species has its turn to feed, without overcrowding.

☐ So it is that the cardinalfishes (Apogonidae family) are not usually seen by the daylight diver unless he searches the darker areas of the reef. A sharp eye will discover some of the more common cardinalfishes (the barred cardinal or the flamefish) sharing a dark reef hole or burrow with a few squirrelfishes or sweepers. Like most night-roaming fishes, the cardinals are handsomely colored in tones of red or bronze. This dark coloration allows them to forage at night without being seen, while their large eyes are adept at spotting zooplankton on the darkened reef.

☐ Certain West Atlantic cardinalfishes have been observed sheltering close to starfishes and sea anemones, apparently for protection from predators. The freckled

Flamefish *Apogon maculatus* To 4 inches. A beautiful, flame-red little fish, one of the most familiar and common cardinals over (and under) West Atlantic reefs. Frequently seen in shallow water floating in the mouths of caves and crevices. Males have been seen carrying eggs in their mouths. **Range:** New England, Bahamas, Bermuda and Florida to Brazil, including the Gulf of Mexico. **Edibility:** poor.

Whitestar cardinalfish *Apogon lachneri* To about 2½ inches. This fish is well-named, for the tiny white spot on the back seems to gleam starlike in the 35 to 200 foot depths preferred by the whitestar. Also taken occasionally in 12 feet of water. **Range:** Bahamas and southern Florida to Venezuela, including the Gulf of Mexico. **Edibility:** poor.

Barred cardinalfish *Apogon binotatus* To 5 inches. A fairly common cardinalfish, reported by Bohlke and Chaplin as being abundant in the Bahamas, and by Walter Starck as frequent at Alligator Reef, Florida. It seems to be capable of changing its color from pale salmon to dark red. Longley working in the Tortugas noted that when over a light background the fish switches instantly to the pallid color phase. Ranges in depth from near-shore to 160 feet. **Range:** Bermuda, Bahamas and Florida to Venezuela. **Edibility:** poor.

Belted cardinalfish *Apogon townsendi* To 2½ inches. A brilliant and iridescent little cardinal, distinctive for the very broad band near the tail with black vertical margins. Younger fish display only the black marginal stripes of this band, which gradually fill in with pigment to become one band, as the fish matures. Taken from near-shore to 90 foot depths. **Range:** Bahamas and Florida to Venezuela. **Edibility:** poor.

Twospot cardinalfish *Apogon pseudomaculatus* To 3½ inches. Somewhat like the flamefish, but notable for being the only cardinal in our area with a small black spot near the tail. A deep water fish ranging from 50 to over 1300 foot depths. A mouth-brooder. **Range:** New England, Bermuda, Bahamas and Florida south to Brazil, including the Gulf of Mexico. **Edibility:** poor.

Freckled cardinalfish *Phaeoptyx conklini* To 3½ inches. There are three closely-related species of distinctively spotted or freckled West Atlantic cardinalfishes that have recently been placed in the genus *Phaeoptyx.* They include the freckled cardinalfish shown here, the sponge cardinalfish (*P. xenus*) and the dusky cardinalfish (*P. pigmentaria*). Due to their spotted coloration, they are often difficult to distinguish underwater. All three species appear to have unusual preferences in the selection of habitats—the sponge cardinal seeks shelter during the day in the central cavity of cylindrical sponges, while the dusky cardinal has been seen sheltering in or near the spines of sea urchins. The freckled cardinalfish has been observed off the Florida Keys hovering around the basket starfish *Astrophyton muricatum* when it is expanded at night. **Range of all three cardinalfishes:** Bahamas and Florida to Venezuela. **Edibility:** poor.

cardinalfish has been observed off the Florida Keys hovering around the basket starfish, *Astrophyton muricatum*, when it is expanded at night. Although cardinalfishes do not have immunity from the stinging tentacles of sea anemones, recently the bridle cardinalfish, *Apogon auro-lineatus*, and the sawcheek cardinalfish, *Apogon quadri-*

squamatus (not shown), were sighted sheltering closely to the deadly tentacles of Caribbean sea anemones. Apparently the protection from predators offered by the host outweighs the danger of being stung and eaten by the anemones. Most cardinals are mouthbrooders that take their eggs into their large mouths for incubation. In most cases, but not all, it is the father who takes this responsibility. The eggs are usually contained in a compact ball, and may number tens of thousands. This very close care and nurturing of the developing eggs, compared with other fish species which allow the eggs to drift with the ocean tides, assures that many more cardinalfishes hatch and grow to maturity.

Conchfish *Astrapogon stellatus* To 3 inches. This rather drab little fish lives as a commensal within the mantle cavity of the live queen conch *Strombas gigas*. As many as five conchfish have been taken from a single conch. They remain in the conch by day, and emerge at night to feed on shrimps, sea lice and other crustaceans. What service they provide to the conch, if any, is not known. The single row of dots running back from pectoral fin to tail is distinctive. **Range:** Bermuda, Bahamas and Florida Keys to Brazil. **Edibility:** poor.

Punctate cardinalfish *Astrapogon puncticulatus* To 3 inches. Closely related to the conchfish, this cardinal is so similar that the two were thought to be the same fish until recently. This fish has never been found in a queen conch, however, and seems to prefer dead shells, rocks and holes in the reef. For differences, note the more pronounced lines radiating from the eye of the punctate and the lack of the distinct line of dots found on the conchfish. **Range:** Florida and the Bahamas to Venezuela. **Edibility:** poor.

SQUIRRELFISHES, SOLDIERFISHES

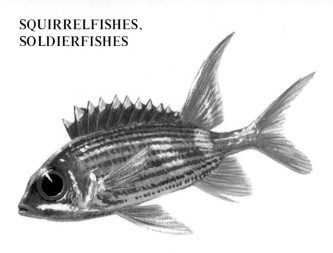

Squirrelfish (candil) *Holocentrus rufus* To 12½ inches. Ranges from shore to about 100 foot depths. Note white spots at tips of dorsal fin spines. This fish and the longjaw are distinctive for the elongated upper tail fin lobes. **Range:** Carolinas, Bermuda, Bahamas, Florida throughout Caribbean. **Edibility:** good.

The holocentrids, commonly known as squirrelfishes or soldierfishes, are primarily nocturnal animals with large, squirrel-like eyes and red coloration. During the day most of the squirrels hide in or near their crevices on the reef bottom. They become active at night, when their dark red hues make them almost invisible, and their keen eyes enable them to forage across the dark reef for shrimps, crabs and other crustaceans. They are very rough, spiny, prickly fishes, not attractive meals to bigger fishes, and most squirrels possess a sharp spine at the base of the gill cover with which they can inflict painful, sometimes poisonous wounds. Most squirrels are not much used for food due to their small size and spiny bodies. The blackbar and cardinal soldierfishes do not have the spiny, prickly bodies of other squirrels and are good food fishes, although rather small in size (to 8½ inches).

☐ Although noted for their shyness during the daytime hours, the secretive squirrels are not difficult to locate for the sharp-eyed diver. Longjaw squirrels are commonly seen by day lurking in or near their reef holes, often in the company of a few blackbar soldierfishes, cardinalfishes, bigeyes or sweepers. Certain West Atlantic squirrels have been found to be rather noisy fishes, much like the croakers. Scientists of the Tektite II Man-In-The-Sea Project recorded a surprising array of squirrelfish sounds, ranging from staccatos and chirps (by the longjaw squirrel) to quacks and a "squeaking door sound" (by the longspine squirrelfish). Their reasons for making these sounds is still not clear, but they may be a component of aggressive action, flight or courtship activity.

Longjaw squirrelfish (candil) *Holocentrus ascensionis* To 2 feet. Quite common, often seen skulking about outer patch reefs. Note greenish dorsal fin, longer upper lobe of tail fin. **Range:** New York, Bermuda, Bahamas, Florida to Brazil, including Gulf of Mexico. **Edibility:** good.

Reef squirrelfish (candil) *Holocentrus coruscus* To 5½ inches. Inhabits coral and rock reefs from shore to 75 foot depths. Note distinctive black spots between first few dorsal fin spines. **Range:** Bermuda, Bahamas, Florida through Lesser Antilles to Venezuela. **Edibility:** poor.

Dusky squirrelfish (candil) *Holocentrus vexillarius* To 6 inches. A common inshore species, found hiding about coral reefs, rocky outcroppings, tidepools. Note black spots between dorsal fin spines. **Range:** New Jersey, Bermuda, Bahamas and Florida through Caribbean, including the Gulf of Mexico. **Edibility:** poor.

113

Longspine squirrelfish (candil) *Holocentrus marianus* To 7 inches. Prefers 50 to 200 foot depths. Note very long third anal fin spine. **Range:** Carolinas, Bahamas through the Caribbean. **Edibility:** poor.

Cardinal soldierfish (candil) *Plectrypops retrospinis* To 5 inches. A secretive fish, preferring patch reefs over 30 to 80 foot depths. A uniformly red fish. **Range:** Bermuda, Bahamas, Florida through the Caribbean. **Edibility:** poor.

Blackbar soldierfish (candil de piedra) *Myripristis jacobus* To 8½ inches. Occasionally seen by divers drifting just inside reef holes and crevices. A handsome fish. **Range:** both sides of Atlantic. In West Atlantic from Bahamas and Florida to Brazil, including the Gulf of Mexico. **Edibility:** good.

114

BIGEYES, SWEEPERS AND BOGAS

Copper sweeper, glassy sweeper *Pempheris schomburgki* To 6 inches. **Range:** Bermuda, the Bahamas and Florida to Brazil. **Edibility:** poor.

Sweepers of the family Pempheridae are cave and crevice dwellers by day, and it is a real delight to discover a small school of these handsome coppery fishes peering out of their grotto. They make strange bobbing movements as they float, caused by vibration of their pectoral fins. Juvenile copper sweepers are tiny, glassy, transparent beauties with opercles and organs of the body cavity glittering iridescent silver with copper and blue reflections. The vertebrae are heavily pigmented with red and black. The iris of the eye is powdered densely with golden bronze and the lips are lemon yellow. William Beebe and John Tee-Van repeatedly sighted a large school of several thousand sweeper juveniles, all barely an inch long, transparent and floating six fathoms down in an open grotto off Bermuda. The "glassy sweeper" gets its name from this juvenile phase. As the fish matures, it assumes the coppery color shown in this 5-inch adult.

☐ Bigeyes, also known as catalufas, are nocturnal fishes like the sweepers, squirrelfishes and cardinalfishes, and they are occasionally found by day sharing a reef cave or grotto with these fishes. Like the squirrels, the bigeyes (family Priacanthidae) are most active at night when they actively stalk such prey as small fishes, crustaceans and polychaete worms, as well as zooplankton in the night tides. They are not entirely nocturnal, however. Investigations show that the stomachs of bigeyes often contain fresh food items during daylight hours.

Glasseye, glasseye snapper *Priacanthus cruentatus* To 1 foot. **Range:** circumtropical; in the West Atlantic, from Bermuda, Bahamas and Florida to Brazil. **Edibility:** fair.

Bigeye *Priacanthus arenatus* To 15 inches. **Range:** both sides of the Atlantic; in the West Atlantic from New England and Bermuda to Argentina, including the Gulf of Mexico. **Edibility:** fair.

☐ Bogas, or bonnetmouths are small, open-water school-ing fishes of the family Emmelichthyidae. They are very fast swimmers, difficult to catch, and they seem to prefer 30 to 150 foot depths, thus little is known of their life cycle. They possess very protrusible upper jaws (hence the name "bonnet mouth" used in the West Indies) well-adapted to plankton feeding. Great schools of bogas appear occasionally off the Cuban coast, usually in the month of December.

Short bigeye *Pristigenys alta* To 11 inches. **Range:** New Eng-land, Bermuda, Florida south through the Antilles, including the Gulf of Mexico. **Edibility:** fair.

Boga, bonnetmouth *Inermia vittata* To 9 inches. **Range:** Ba-hamas and Florida to Venezuela. **Edibility:** fair.

MOJARRAS, TRIPLETAILS, HAWKFISHES

Yellowfin mojarra (mojarra de casta) *Gerres cinereus* To 15 inches. **Range:** both Atlantic and Pacific Coasts; in the West Atlantic, from Bermuda, the Bahamas and Florida to Brazil, including the Gulf of Mexico. **Edibility:** fair.

Mojarras, of the family Gerridae, are familiar fishes to divers in the West Indies since they are often hovering nearby, especially over sandy bottom, shallow water areas. They are curious fishes, and their large, jet-black eyes set in pale, silvery bodies seem to follow the diver about the reef. They feed on such small invertebrates as worms, mollusks, crabs and shrimps, which they dig out of the sand with their protrusible mouths. They are adept at changing color, and their bodies can flash from silver over sandy bottom to striped green-brown over weedy areas.

□ The tripletail is so-named for the extended lobes of the dorsal and anal fins, giving it the appearance of having three tails. Tripletails, of the family Lobotidae are found in brackish and fresh water inlets as well as in inshore reef environments. These fishes have the surprising ability, especially as juveniles, of "playing dead," apparently to deter predators. They turn sideways and float on the surface, and manage to look very much like dead leaves floating on the water. They are fished, especially in warmer months, around docks and jetties, buoys and wrecks.

☐ Hawkfishes of the family Cirrhitidae, get their avian name from their habit of perching in the branches of coral heads or in rocky crevices, and swooping rapidly on smaller fishes and crustaceans. Hawkfishes will sit for hours in motionless vigil, punctuated by sudden dashes for food. Although numerous species of hawks are common in the Indo-Pacific, only one species is known from the tropical Western Atlantic—the red-spotted hawkfish. It is a common sight to see this red-speckled predator sitting boldly out in the open or nestled in a coral clump, waiting for a meal to swim by.

Redspotted hawkfish *Amblycirrhitus pinos* To 3½ inches. **Range:** Bahamas and Florida south through the Antilles to Central America. **Edibility:** poor.

Tripletail (viajaca de la mar) *Lobotes surinamensis* To 40 inches. Usually dark brown in color, but pale, greenish and cream yellow individuals have been taken. **Range:** circumtropical; in the West Atlantic, from New England, Bermuda, the Bahamas and Florida south to Argentina, including the Gulf of Mexico. **Edibility:** good.

TARPON, BONEFISHES, LADYFISHES, HERRINGS, SHAD

Tarpon (sabalo) *Megalops atlantica* To 8 feet. **Range:** both sides of Atlantic; in the West Atlantic from Nova Scotia to Brazil, including the Gulf of Mexico. **Edibility:** poor.

A June moon may mean one thing to lovers, but for the compulsive tarpon fisherman it has a pull greater than the attraction of star-crossed lovers, or the lure of Las Vegas to the gambler. There is no other game fish in the world that provides such an explosive, dynamic reaction to being hooked as the tarpon. Dedicated anglers leave families and jobs for the awesome experience of hooking into 40 to 200 pounds of silver-plated violence. Tarpon havens abound throughout Florida, the Bahamas, the Caribbean, and the Gulf of Mexico. One mecca for tarpon fishermen is Florida's Boca Grande Pass.

☐ At a time known to fishermen as the "big tides," when the moon reaches its first full phase in June, it strikes a position with relation to earth and sun that causes the waters of Charlotte Harbor to race out rapidly through Boca Grande. Millions of baitfishes, shrimp, crabs, and other crustaceans are swept into the hungry mouths of waiting tarpon. The scene above water is chaotic, as boatloads of wide-eyed fishermen jockey into position for a chance to hook into a tarpon. In spite of all the preparation, many a beginner has been known to "freeze"

120

when the great silver king approaches the boat. And when 3 to 6 feet of fury explodes from the water, *any* angler can be unnerved.

☐ Tarpon, of the family Elopidae, have no real food value, and out of consideration for the nobility of this lordly fish, few people ever kill one. They are usually released to strike another day. A peculiar characteristic of the tarpon is the habit of "rolling" on the ocean's surface. Tarpon have a lung-like gas bladder and the rolling helps them take in atmospheric air. One angler tells of a fishing trip in a primitive lagoon in the outback of Yucatan. When he asked the Mexican charterboat captain if there were any fish in the lagoon, the captain motioned him up the mast. When he climbed to the top of the mast, he gulped hard. He saw fishes rolling as far as the eye could see—literally miles of tarpon rolling in silvery splendor. A number of 200 pound tarpon have been taken by fishermen, but the record is an 8 foot giant that weighed an estimated 340 pounds.

☐ Tarpon and bonefishes are among the most primitive of living bony fishes. Both have a long, deeply forked tail and a single dorsal fin of soft rays. Bonefishes of the family Albulidae are targets of the light tackle game fishermen. They combine a wariness that can unnerve the most patient angler with incredible speed and power when hooked. Large expanses of water around the Florida Keys, the Bahamas, the Gulf of Mexico and numerous islands of the Caribbean consist of wide stretches of shallow-water flats, varying from white ocean sand to shallow creek beds to thick turtle-grass and mangrove-choked bays and sounds. This is bonefish country, and skiff fishermen pole patiently, stalking "bones" through polarized sunglasses. Even a modest-sized bonefish will make the line disappear from the spool so fast when it strikes that beginning anglers are often left with a snapped and empty line before they realize that the bone has come and gone. Only the permit approaches the incredible long-run capacity of the wily bonefish. Closely related to the tarpon, the ten-pounder or ladyfish of the family Elopidae occurs around the world in tropical seas. It, too, is a resident of shallow, brackish lagoons. The ladyfish also leaps and struggles when hooked, but is a pale shadow of a fighter compared with the bonefish or tarpon.

121

□ To see a school of sardines, anchovies or herrings move through the underwater world is to see a perfectly co-ordinated *corps de ballet*—hundreds, even thousands, of silvery projectiles moving through the water as a single unit, in perfect unison and beauty. All of the herrings of the family Clupeidae are noted for their oily flesh. Economically they form one of the world's most important groups of food fishes, not just for man, but as a vast food reservoir for larger fishes. Other important members of the clupeid family include the menhaden, which is used extensively to produce fishmeal, the shad and the alewife, found from Nova Scotia to Florida. Anchovies, of the family Engraulidae, look and act much like small, round herrings with one important difference. All of the 100 or so species of anchovies are instantly recognizeable by their small, shark-like lower jaw set far back on the underside of the head. Anchovies are tremendously valuable as food for humans, as well as for live and frozen bait. Their greatest abundance is in tropical marine waters.

Bonefish (macabi) *Albula vulpes* To 3½ feet. **Range:** worldwide in tropical seas; in the West Atlantic from New England to southeastern Brazil, including the Gulf of Mexico. **Edibility:** poor.

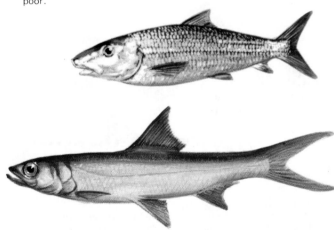

Ladyfish, tenpounder (matezuelo real) *Elops saurus* To 3 feet. **Range:** New England to Brazil, including the Gulf of Mexico. **Edibility:** poor.

122

Atlantic thread herring (machuelo) *Opisthonema oglinum* To 12 inches. **Range:** New England and Bermuda to southeastern Brazil, including the Gulf of Mexico. **Edibility:** poor.

Dwarf herring *Jenkinsia lamprotaenia* To 3½ inches. **Range:** Bermuda, Bahamas and Florida to Venezuela, including the Gulf of Mexico. **Edibility:** poor.

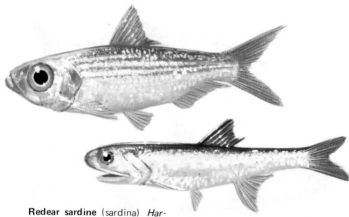

Redear sardine (sardina) *Harengula humeralis* To 9 inches. **Range:** Bermuda, Bahamas and Florida to Brazil, including the Gulf of Mexico. **Edibility:** good. Used for food and bait throughout West Indies.

Dusky anchovy (anchoa) *Anchoa lyolepis* To 3 inches. **Range:** Greater and Lesser Antilles, and the Gulf of Mexico. **Edibility:** good. Also used extensively as fishermen's bait.

123

American shad, white shad *Alosa sapidissima* To 30 inches. The anadromous shad lives most of its life at sea. Spawning brings them into rivers each year. They have suffered heavily from dams, pollution and overfishing. **Range:** St. Lawrence River to Florida. A very close relative, the hickory shad (*A. mediocris*) ranges from the Gulf of Maine to Florida, and is more dominant in southern waters. **Edibility:** American shad— excellent; hickory shad—poor (roe is excellent).

Alewife *Alosa pseudoharengus* To 14 inches. Very similar to the shad and menhaden, but with a larger eye. Formerly of substantial commercial importance, it is much less so today. The meat is bony and of poor quality. The roe is excellent. **Range:** Labrador to Florida. **Edibility:** see above.

Atlantic menhaden *Brevoortia tyrannus* To 18 inches. An important commercial fish, over 2 billion pounds were taken in the U.S. in 1960, used mostly for animal and poultry feeds. Also used heavily as a chum and bait fish. **Range:** Nova Scotia to northern Florida and the Gulf of Mexico. **Edibility:** poor.

124

COBIAS, SNOOKS, SEA CATFISHES

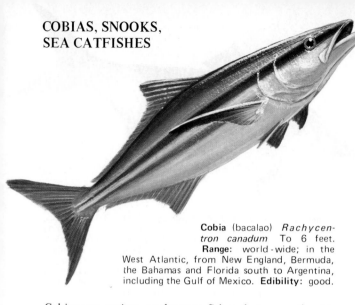

Cobia (bacalao) *Rachycentron canadum* To 6 feet.
Range: world-wide; in the West Atlantic, from New England, Bermuda, the Bahamas and Florida south to Argentina, including the Gulf of Mexico. **Edibility:** good.

Cobias are roving, predaceous fishes that range the Atlantic from Massachusetts to Argentina. They are found well offshore, and inshore around inlets, bays and mangrove sloughs, where they feed on crabs, shrimps, fishes, and squids. Gulf Coast charterboat fishermen react strangely when the cobia, or ling is sighted. They thump the sides of the boat, splash water with rods and oars, ring bells, or turn the boat in tight, noisy circles. This activity would frighten off most fishes, but the cobia seems to need excitement and noise to get into a feeding mood. At the peak of the noise-making a pair of cobia may suddenly explode into action and take the bait for a series of 70 or 80-yard runs. Ten to 15 pound cobia are frequently caught from beach piers. Twenty-five to 30 pound fish are caught in marginal offshore waters. Big 50, 60 and 70 pound giants may be had in the offshore blue. One 5' 10" cobia was taken off Virginia that weighed 102 pounds. The cobia, of the family Rachycentridae, occurs around the world in warm waters.

☐ Snooks or robalos of the family Centropomidae are shovel-nosed fishes frequently found inshore in mangrove sloughs and river mouths. While snorkeling near shore in 3 feet of water off Pompano Beach, Florida, I poked my nose into a rock grotto and came eyeball-to-eyeball with a 3 foot snook. I am not sure who was more surprised, but the snook came bursting out of the grotto over my right shoulder to disappear in a froth of bubbles and snook wake.

☐ Four species of snook are known from the Caribbean and a fifth from the Gulf of Mexico. The common snook shown here grows to be the largest in the West Atlantic, reaching 4½ feet in length. It is an excellent food fish, with delicate, white flaky flesh, not unlike that of the striped bass.

☐ The sea catfish, or "hardhead," which ranges from Cape Cod to the West Indies and throughout the Gulf of Mexico, gets a very low rating as a gamefish. The gafftopsail catfish, however, is gaining a sizeable following on the Gulf Coast as a fine gamefish and an excellent food fish (the flesh is white, firm and tasty). In Texas it has acquired the nickname "tourist trout," and when the gafftops are running, people who live hundreds of miles

Snook (robalo) *Centropomus undecimalis* To 4½ feet. **Range:** South Carolina to Brazil, including the Gulf of Mexico. **Edibility:** excellent.

inland swarm to the coast for the action. Veteran Gulf Coast anglers say that when the gafftops make their initial appearance each spring as the water begins to warm, the Spanish mackerel, king mackerel, cobia (ling) and pompano will not be far behind. Both the sea and gafftopsail catfishes belong to the Ariidae family, and they are mouthbrooders, like the cardinalfishes. The male fish carries from 50 to 60 large (½" to 1" diameter) eggs in his mouth until they hatch some 9 weeks later. Even after they hatch, he nurtures them in his mouth for an additional two to four weeks, until they are about 3" long and ready for independence. During this entire 11 to 13-week period, the male catfish goes without food.

Sea catfish, hardhead (bagre) *Arius felis* **To 1½ feet. Range:** Cape Cod south through the Antilles and throughout the Gulf of Mexico. **Edibility:** poor.

Gafftopsail catfish (bagre) *Bagre marinus* **To 2 feet. Range:** Cape Cod to Panama and throughout the Gulf of Mexico. **Edibility:** good.

127

BLUEFISHES, TILEFISHES, REMORAS

Bluefish, tailor, snapper (anchoa) *Pomatomus saltatrix* To 4 feet. **Range:** world-wide in tropical and temperate seas. **Edibility:** good, but spoils quickly. Must be eaten fresh.

Bluefishes are fast-moving, schooling fishes with a reputation for bloodthirsty feeding habits that outstrip those of the jacks and barracuda. Not unlike the piranha, the bluefish is an animated chopping machine that preys heavily on other fishes. The bluefish, of the family Pomatomidae, is a favorite with fishermen, both shore and offshore, for its fighting quality and its excellent taste. Young juveniles, often called tailors or snappers, are common inshore. One characteristic by which bluefish may be distinguished from similar fishes is the black blotch at the base of the pectoral fin.

□ The sand tilefish is an interesting, industrious animal with a unique talent for constructing burrows around the reef. Scientists of the Tektite I and II Man-In-The-Sea Projects observed and documented the bird-like nest building activity of the tilefish. The fish first excavates a trench in the sand bottom of the reef, over which it constructs intricate walls and a roof of coral debris and shell fragments. Here the fish hovers, just a few inches off the bottom, plunging headfirst into its burrow when disturbed. In one experiment, Tektite divers marked and then scattered from 500 to 600 fragments of a tilefish's burrow. Upon returning, the tilefish began putting his house in order. Within 8 days he had rebuilt his burrow, using 460 of the original coral and shell fragments.

☐ The common tilefish is another interesting member of the family Branchiostegidae. First introduced to the New England market in 1879, this tilefish was an immediate commercial success. Shortly after, disaster struck the vast tilefish schools that ranged from New England to the Virginia Capes. Millions of dead tilefish were reported, and one ship sailed through 150 miles of them. Estimates of mortality ranged up to 1½ billion fish. Scientists explained that unseasonal Arctic gales and ice had suddenly chilled the water, making it too cold for the tilefish. It was 10 years before any more tilefish were taken, and then only 8 individuals were caught. Gradually, however, the fish reestablished itself, until recently, when 1,238,500 pounds were taken.

☐ The remora or sharksucker is the well-known hitchhiker of the sea. By means of a laminated disc on the top of its head, the remora clamps itself firmly to almost any available host and takes a free ride. Sharks are popular hosts, but remoras are not fussy. They are found attached to whales, marlin, groupers, rays, boats, timbers and other floating objects. Various species of remoras ap-

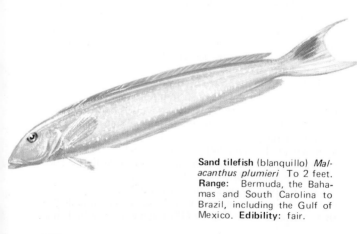

Sand tilefish (blanquillo) *Malacanthus plumieri* To 2 feet. **Range:** Bermuda, the Bahamas and South Carolina to Brazil, including the Gulf of Mexico. **Edibility:** fair.

pear to be always associated with the same kind of host. Some species are found only on billfishes, while others are at home only on barracudas. Incredibly, remoras have been used as "living fishhooks" by various primitive tribes the world over. A line is tied to the tail of the remora and it is thrown overboard in the vicinity of a large turtle. When it attaches itself to the turtle, fishermen play the turtle near to the boat, and it is captured. The Arawak Indians of southern Cuba, Venezuelan Indians, Australian aborigines and numerous other tribes used the remora in this ingenious way.

Common tilefish *Lopholatilus chamaeleonticeps* To 2½ feet. **Range:** Nova Scotia to the Gulf of Mexico. **Edibility:** good.

Sharksucker, remora, suckerfish (pegador) *Echeneis naucrates* To 3½ feet. **Range:** circumtropical; in the West Atlantic, from New England and Bermuda to Uruguay, including the Gulf of Mexico. **Edibility:** poor.

130

BARRACUDA, SILVERSIDES, MULLETS AND THREADFINS

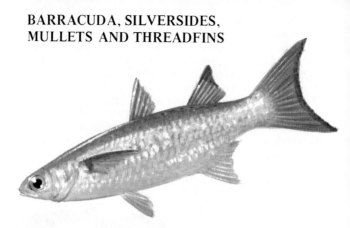

White mullet, black mullet, fatback, jumper (lisa blanca, liseta) *Mugil curema* To 3 feet. **Range:** both sides of the Atlantic; in the West Atlantic, from New England to southeastern Brazil, including the Gulf of Mexico. **Edibility:** good.

Vast, silvery clouds of silversides and mullets school, race and leap in Western Atlantic coastal shallows, providing a movable feast for such predators as barracuda, jacks, mackerel and man. The torpedo-shaped mullet ranks as a leading food fish in Florida, where it is called the "black mullet." They are so rich in oil they can be fried in their own fat. Also called "fatbacks" and "jumpers," mullets are expert at leaping out of the water to escape nets, predators, and seemingly just for the pure joy of jumping. At certain times of the day, coastal shallows, bays and inlets are often alive with leaping mullets. Members of the family Mugilidae, mullets are bottom grubbers, fond of sucking up mouthfuls of bottom sand and filtering out small plants and animals. Since they are basically herbivorous, they rarely take a hook unless it is baited with bread or dough. They are frequently caught in nets.

☐ Silversides (family Atherinidae) are named for their brilliant, flashing lateral stripe, and they share with mullets such characteristics as divided dorsal fins, pelvic fins placed in the middle of the abdomen, small, weakly-toothed mouths and tasty, oily flesh. Often scooped out of the sea and cooked over spits on the beach, they pro-

131

vide such delicious fare that Mexican and Caribbean gourmets call them *pescado del rey*, "fish for a king." Strangely for schooling fishes, silverside fry start life shy and antisocial. Studies at New York's American Museum of Natural History indicate that quarter - inch hatchlings avoid each other. Half-inchers may aggregate a few seconds, but avoid meeting head-on. At three-quarters of an inch, 10 fry may assemble in a ragged formation. From then on they school easily and with increasing discipline. A well-known relative is the California grunion silverside (*Lueresthes tenuis*) which rides waves ashore to mate and spawn on the beach.

☐ Nothing is more disconcerting to the diver than the specter of a 1 or 2 foot barracuda following closely and watchfully as the diver makes his rounds of the reefs. In Florida and Caribbean waters, the "friendly" barracuda (family Sphyraenidae) is almost inescapable in some areas. The wise diver soon gives up trying to chase them away (they quickly return anyway) and welcomes them along as companions on his tour. They are quite harmless and seem content to follow the diver curiously, as though waiting for a handout. Most of the recorded attacks by the "ferocious" barracuda occurred when the fish was speared, boated or trapped, at which time most fishes will bite anything. Some barracuda attacks have occurred in murky water, when visibility was poor, and

Fantail mullet (lisa) *Mugil trichodon* To 18 inches. **Range:** Bermuda, Bahamas and Florida to Brazil, including the Gulf of Mexico. **Edibility:** good.

Smallscale threadfin (barbudo) *Polydactylus oligodon* To 16 inches. **Range:** Bahamas and Florida to Brazil. **Edibility:** good.

132

presumably the fish mistook an arm or leg for a small fish. Divers wearing shiny metal objects would do well to remove them in the presence of barracuda. They have been known to strike at shiny objects, apparently mistaking them for the flash of a small fish's side or belly. Although adult barracuda tend to be solitary hunters, smaller ones have been observed in schools, herding smaller fishes into compact groups. They will cut a swath through the group, snapping at and killing their prey by the score. Then they return and eat the stunned or maimed fish at their leisure. Barracuda are excellent game fish, capable of providing all the battle a sport fisherman can handle. Small barracuda make excellent eating, but large ones in the West Indies rank with the amberjack in causing ciguatera poisoning (see page 39).

☐ Threadfins of the family Polynemidae are much like mullets, but the unique pectoral fins are split into two parts, the lower of which is composed of 7 or 8 thread-like rays. Threadfins probe into sand and mud bottoms with these rays, and they probably serve both tactile and chemoreceptor functions. The mouth is under a pronounced, pig-like snout. They are beautiful silvery fishes when seen underwater, often swimming with sand drums and palometas over sandy beach areas.

Great barracuda (picuda) *Sphyraena barracuda* To 10 feet. Rare over 5 feet. Contrary to popular belief, attacks by barracuda on man are very rare. **Range:** world-wide; in the West Atlantic, from New England to Brazil, including the Gulf of Mexico. **Edibility:** small fish (2-3 pounds) good. Larger fish may carry ciguatera toxin (see page 39).

Southern sennet (picudilla) *Sphyraena picudilla* To 18 inches. This small barracuda and the similar "guaguanche" (*S. guachancho*) are reported to be good eating, and have not been implicated in ciguatera poisoning. **Range:** *S. picudilla:* Bermuda, Bahamas and Florida to Uruguay. *S. guachancho:* New England to Brazil, including the Gulf of Mexico. **Edibility:** see above.

Hardhead silverside, blue fry *Atherinomorous stipes* To 5 inches. **Range:** Bahamas and Florida to Brazil. **Edibility:** good.

Reef silverside, blue fry *Allanetta harringtonensis* To 3 inches. **Range:** Bermuda, Bahamas, Florida through the West Indies, including the Gulf of Mexico. **Edibility:** good.

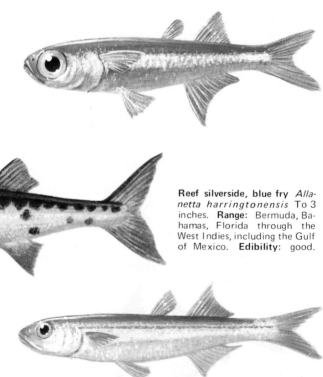

134

CODS AND HAKES

Atlantic cod *Gadus morhua* To 6 feet. **Range:** Arctic seas south to Virginia. **Edibility:** excellent.

These cold and temperate water bottom fishes are vitally important to the world's food supply and they support huge, centuries-old fisheries on both sides of the Atlantic. The profitable codfish pulled Europeans across the North Atlantic by the shipload to settle New World shores. So paramount was the common cod to the settlers of New England that it was placed on the colonial seal of Massachusetts. Its popularity as a basic food fish has not diminished. The Grand Banks off Newfoundland and the coastal shelves of Greenland still attract the fishing fleets of the world in search of succulent, nutritious cods and hakes. Fishermen take nearly 150 million pounds of haddock every year, making it a leading East Coast food fish. The annual commercial take of pollock, another member of the cod family, is nearly 10 million pounds. Commercial fishermen use large trawling nets, set lines, seines and gill nets. Because the flesh keeps so well, dried and salted cod may be shipped to any part of the world.

Haddock *Melanogrammus aeglefinus* To 44 inches. **Range:** Greenland to Virginia. **Edibility:** excellent.

☐ Almost all of North America's 24 species of cods and hakes are marine fishes. Members of the family Gadidae, they are omnivorous and they roam sand and rock bottoms 100 to 1500 feet down, preying in voracious packs upon crustaceans, mollusks, fishes, worms and vegetation. Codfishes and their relatives may be distinguished by the "cod look," partly due to the fact that the ventral fins are placed ahead of the pectoral fins, often under the throat. They all possess soft-rayed fins, usually without spines.

Pollock *Pollachius virens* To 3½ feet. **Range:** Gulf of St. Lawrence to Virginia. **Edibility:** excellent.

Silver hake *Merluccius bilinearis* To 3 feet. **Range:** Gulf of St. Lawrence to South Carolina. **Edibility:** good.

Red hake, squirrel hake *Urophycis chuss* To 2½ feet. **Range:** Gulf of St. Lawrence to North Carolina. **Edibility:** poor.

FLATFISHES

Ocellated flounder *Ancylopsetta quadrocellata* To 10 inches.
Range: Maryland to Florida and the Gulf of Mexico. **Edibility:** good.

If you see what appears to be a flying carpet with fins and a white underside rippling about the reef, gliding to the bottom to disappear into the sand, you are watching a flatfish. The flatfishes include many of the world's tastiest and most valuable food fishes, such as the sole, flounder, halibut, sanddab, turbot, and plaice. All flatfishes begin life much like any other symmetrical fish, with an eye on either side of the head. Within a few days, however, one eye starts migrating toward the other, and soon both eyes are close together on the upper side of the animals' body. The mouth becomes strangely twisted, and the dorsal fin grows forward on the fish, almost reaching the mouth. These unusual developments prepare the fish for its bottom-dwelling existence. Within a few more days, the young flatfish sinks to the ocean bottom, where it spends the rest of its life lying on its blind side (which is usually white), with the eyed side up. American flatfishes are separated into two broad categories. One of these includes the Bothidae and Pleuronectidae (flounders, halibuts, whiffs, sanddabs and soles), the other is the Soleidae and Cynoglossidae (broadsoles and tonguefishes). The Bothidae are left-eyed flounders (so called because their eyes are on the left side of the head) and the Pleuronectidae are right-eye flounders. Most flatfishes have a remarkable facility to change their colors to match the bottom. Their excellent camouflage is aided by their ability to quickly bury themselves in the bottom sand and they are extremely difficult to locate by an untrained eye. Most are carnivorous fishes that dash out of hiding to gobble down smaller fishes and crustaceans. They range in size from only a few inches to great, flat 10-foot giants weighing 700 pounds. Biologists recently discovered an unassuming little sole in the Red Sea (*Pardachirus marmoratus*) that appears to carry a highly effective shark repellent. Repeated tests demonstrate that sharks refuse to bite the sole, and the fish is being closely studied to see if the repellant can be isolated for use by man.

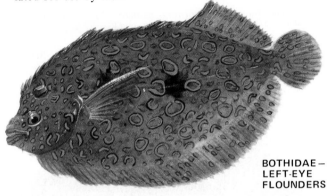

BOTHIDAE — LEFT-EYE FLOUNDERS

Peacock flounder (arreves) *Bothus lunatus* To 18 inches. **Range:** Bermuda, Bahamas and Florida to Brazil. **Edibility:** good.

Bay whiff *Citharichthys spilopterus* To 8 inches. **Range:** New Jersey to Brazil, including the Gulf of Mexico. **Edibility:** fair.

Southern flounder *Paralichthys lethostigma* To 2½ feet. **Range:** North Carolina to Texas. **Edibility:** good.

Summer flounder *Paralichthys dentatus* To 2½ feet. **Range:** Maine to South Carolina. **Edibility:** good.

Eyed flounder (arreves) *Bothus ocellatus* To 6½ inches. **Range:** New York and Bermuda to Brazil, including the Gulf of Mexico. **Edibility:** poor.

PLEURONECTIDAE — RIGHT-EYE FLOUNDERS

Winter flounder *Pseudopleuronectes americanus* To 1½ feet. **Range:** Labrador to North Carolina. **Edibility:** excellent.

Naked sole, zebra sole (arreves) *Gymnachirus melas* To 6 inches. **Range:** Massachusetts to Bahamas, Florida and the Gulf of Mexico. **Edibility:** poor.

Hogchoker *Trinectes maculatus* To 9 inches. **Range:** Massachusetts to Panama and the Gulf of Mexico. **Edibility:** poor.

CYNOGLOSSIDAE — TONGUEFISHES

Caribbean tonguefish *Symphurus arawak* To 2 inches. **Range:** Florida Keys and throughout Caribbean Sea. **Edibility:** poor.

140

SURGEONS, TANGS

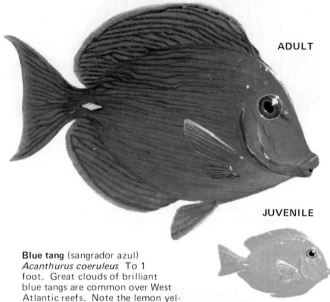

ADULT

JUVENILE

Blue tang (sangrador azul)
Acanthurus coeruleus To 1
foot. Great clouds of brilliant
blue tangs are common over West
Atlantic reefs. Note the lemon yel-
low juvenile. Pre-adults may be part blue and part yellow. Blue
fishes with yellow tails are common. Separable from the ocean
surgeon and doctorfish by the white sheath on the caudal spine.
Range: New York, Bermuda, Bahamas and Florida to Brazil, including the Gulf of Mexico. **Edibility:** poor.

If, while diving around coral heads, you are suddenly en-
gulfed in a vast, indigo-blue cloud of fishes, you have met
the magnificent blue tangs of the West Atlantic. Large
schools of blue tangs, doctorfishes and ocean surgeons
are common off West Atlantic reefs, and they cover a
wide range from Massachusetts to Brazil and the Gulf of
Mexico. To see one or two hundred of these fishes rising
in an indigo-blue or pale gray storm from a coral head is
a feast for the eyes. The surgeonfishes of the Acanthuridae
family, frequently called tangs or doctorfishes, are so-
named for the scalpel-like spine on either side of the body
just in front of the tail. The spine may be more aptly
compared with a switch-blade knife, since in most surgeons the blade is hinged and lies flat along the body in a
sheath. When called into play, the blade flicks out and

points forward, and by repeatedly sideswiping another fish, the surgeon can cause serious injury. Careless fishermen who are unaware of the blade can receive nasty cuts when handling the resourceful tang. The beginning diver need not worry about being attacked by hordes of surgeonfishes. The tang, or for that matter, any fish, will rarely attack a creature larger than itself. The usual object of attack is another fish, often of the same size and species, that acts as though it may threaten the hold of the first fish on its section of reef or "territory." In its natural reef habitat, the tang has but to give a warning flick of its tail toward an intruder fish, which invariably withdraws. In an aquarium, however, where there is no place to hide, an overly aggressive surgeon can do considerable damage to its tankmates. Like parrotfishes, tangs are herbivorous, continually searching out and cropping the reef algae. A large school of tangs may swoop down on a small coral head and leave it practically bare of algae. They are not much esteemed by fish gourmets because of the strong odor and savor of the flesh.

Doctorfish (sangrador) *Acanthurus chirurgas* To 13½ inches. The doctorfish, like all surgeons, is highly changeable in color, and it can change from deep brown to pale coloration depending on background and lighting. May be easily mistaken for the ocean surgeon, but note the vertical body bars and the more rectangular tail. **Range:** New England, Bermuda, Bahamas, Florida to the hump of Brazil, including the Gulf of Mexico. **Edibility:** poor.

Ocean surgeon (sangrador) *Acanthurus bahianus* To 14 inches. Quite similar in appearance to the doctorfish, and the two are often seen swimming together in feeding aggregations, but the ocean surgeon has a more lunate tail, and no bars on the body. **Range:** New England, Bermuda, Bahamas and Florida to the hump of Brazil, including the Gulf of Mexico. **Edibility:** poor.

TRIGGERFISHES AND FILEFISHES

Queen triggerfish, old wife (cochino) *Balistes vetula* To 2 feet. Unmistakable with its blue-striped head and long, trailing fin filaments. A very intelligent, aggressive animal with a special fondness for sea urchins, particularly *Diadema*. A reef dweller, it also ventures into sand, seagrass and rubble habitats. A good food fish, called "turbot" in the West Indies due to its resemblance to the flatfish when skinned. **Range:** both sides of the Atlantic; in the West Atlantic from New England to southeastern Brazil, including the Gulf of Mexico. **Edibility:** see above.

A close look at the triggerfish of the Balistidae family shows it to be a fascinating, attractive animal with a perky disposition and a peculiar "hide and lock" defense mechanism. Probably because they are such slow swimmers, triggers have developed a number of protective devices. When attacked or frightened, the trigger dives straight for a hole or crevice in the coral and erects its large first dorsal fin, which is locked in place by the second sliding dorsal spine or "trigger." Thus wedged into its hole, there is no way a predator can remove the trigger and it is usually left alone.

☐ Although seemingly grotesquely configured, with their eyes almost in the center of their bodies, the carnivorous triggers are perfectly designed to prey upon prickly crustaceans, mollusks and echinoderms. Triggers are one of the few animals that can attack a spiny sea urchin with impunity. Since their eyes are so far back in their heads, safe from the spines, they can bite the urchin's spines off with their sharp teeth, throw the urchin on its back, and feast on the soft underbelly. Another technique learned by the intelligent trigger to obtain food is the art of using water as a tool. The queen triggerfish has been seen to blow jets of water at the base of a strolling sea urchin, until it is finally bowled over by the force of the jets. Once on its side, the urchin becomes a meal for the hungry trigger. The bodies of triggers are covered with hard, plate-like scales, forming a flexible yet solid armor. The tails of some species are equipped with rows of spines, and they are adept at side-swiping and tail-whipping an enemy.

☐ Very noticeable in balistids is their ability to rotate the eyes independently, enabling them to observe two different scenes at once. They swim by undulating the soft dorsal and anal fins languidly, bringing their tail into action only when speed is required.

Gray triggerfish (cucuyo) *Balistes capriscus* To 1 foot. Found either singly or in small pods over reefs, rocks and hard bottoms. Rare in the West Indies, but more common around Bermuda and higher latitudes. **Range:** Nova Scotia to Argentina, including the Gulf of Mexico. **Edibility:** fair.

Ocean triggerfish *Canthidermis sufflamen* To 2 feet. A large grayish fish, at times almost white, often seen cruising singly over offshore reefs near drop offs to deep water. **Range:** New England south through the Lesser Antilles, including the Gulf of Mexico. **Edibility:** good.

Sargassum triggerfish *Xanthichthys ringens* To 10 inches. One of the most abundant West Indian reef fishes at depths of over 100 feet. Rarely encountered in shallower depths. Juveniles have been taken in floating clumps of sargassum weed. **Range:** uncertain, but thought to be circumtropical; in the West Atlantic, from the Carolinas, Bermuda and the Bahamas south to Venezuela. **Edibility:** poor.

Black durgon *Melichthys niger* To 1½ feet. Common in some areas, such as Bimini and the Bahamas, fairly rare in others. Prefers clear water outer reefs at depths of 50 feet or more. A striking fish. **Range:** circumtropical, in the West Atlantic, from the Bahamas and Florida to Brazil. **Edibility:** poor.

☐ The filefishes of the family Monacanthidae are very closely related to the triggerfishes. They are distinguished by the fact that their first dorsal spine is located well forward, usually over the eye, while on the triggerfish the first dorsal spine is placed well in back of the eye. Filefishes also have much narrower bodies than the triggers and possess a skin that is almost file-like (hence the name), compared to the plate-like scales of the triggers. A common sight on West Atlantic coral reefs is a pair of white spotted filefishes, picking and fluttering about the reef. As with the butterflyfishes, it is not known whether these are always male and female fishes, but they seem very closely attached.

Whitespotted filefish *Cantherhines macrocerus* To 17 inches. Often seen in pairs fluttering daintily about the reef. Limited data indicates that these pairs are male and female fishes. Feeds on such unlikely fare as sponges, hydroids, stinging coral, gorgonions and algae. **Range:** Bermuda, Bahamas and Florida to Brazil. **Edibility:** poor.

Orangespotted filefish, taillight filefish *Cantherhines pullus* To 7½ inches. Distinctive for the orange spots across the body and the 2 white spots at top and bottom of the tail base. Fairly common. When threatened it erects its formidable first dorsal spine. **Range:** New England, Bermuda, Bahamas and Florida to Brazil, including the Gulf of Mexico. **Edibility:** poor.

Fringed filefish *Monacanthus ciliatus* To 8 inches. Look for this filefish hiding (often head down) in beds of turtle grass. An expert color-changer, it can skillfully blend into its sea grass background. **Range:** Newfoundland to Bermuda, Bahamas and Florida to Argentina, including the Gulf of Mexico. **Edibility:** poor.

Pygmy filefish, speckled filefish *Monacanthus setifer* To 7 inches. The adult male (shown) has the second dorsal ray prolonged into a filament. Highly changeable in color to match surroundings. **Range:** North Carolina, Bermuda, Bahamas south through the Caribbean, including the Gulf of Mexico. **Edibility:** poor.

146

Slender filefish *Monacanthus tuckeri* To 3½ inches. Unique due to its slender body, this little filefish has been found over seagrass, patch reefs, rock and sand bottoms, and hiding among gorgonian fronds. **Range:** Carolinas, Bermuda, Bahamas and Florida through the Antilles. **Edibility:** poor.

Orange filefish (cachua perra) *Aluterus schoepfi* To 1½ feet. Distinctive for the tiny orange spots peppered across the body. Found in a variety of habitats, appears to feed on algae and seagrasses. **Range:** Nova Scotia south to Brazil, including the Gulf of Mexico. **Edibility:** poor.

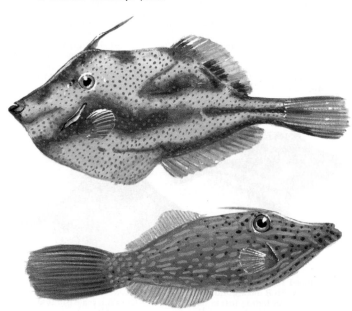

Scrawled filefish *Aluterus scriptus* To 3 feet. Notable for its large size, brilliant blue markings and broom-like tail. Often seen drifting along, head downward, surveying the bottom for food. Known to eat stinging coral, algae, gorgonians, sea anemones and tunicates. **Range:** circumtropical; in the West Atlantic, from Massachusetts to Brazil, including the Gulf of Mexico. **Edibility:** poor.

PUFFERS, PORCUPINEFISHES AND TRUNKFISHES

Bandtail puffer (tambor) *Sphoeroides spengleri* To 1 foot. Common in seagrass beds but also found over patch reefs, sand and coral rubble, usually in shallow water rarely over 25 feet deep. The row of round black spots from chin to tail is distinctive. **Range:** New England, Bermuda, Bahamas and Florida to Brazil, including the Gulf of Mexico. **Edibility:** poor, viscera may be poisonous.

Checkered puffer (tambor) *Sphoeroides testudineus* To 10 inches. A bright-eyed puffer with an orange iris, common in seagrass habitats, mangrove sloughs, and found over a variety of shallow-water reef and sand bottoms. **Range:** New England, Bahamas and Florida to Brazil, including the Gulf of Mexico. **Edibility:** poor, viscera may be poisonous.

When threatened by a predator, a puffer fish sucks in a bellyful of water and almost instantly becomes three times larger. The hungry predator, realizing that the fat little puffer is now too big to fit in its mouth, looks elsewhere for a meal. When removed from the water by curious humans, puffers use the same defense, gulping air instead of water and producing angry grunting noises.

As a result, they frequently become lampshades or mantlepieces in seaside restaurants and the homes of marine collectors. The organs and sometimes the flesh of certain puffers contain a deadly poison, tetrodotoxin. Although it has wide medical application, the poison can kill quickly if eaten, and puffer food poisoning is fatal in 60 percent of the cases. Even so, puffers are eaten with great relish in Japan, in a dish called *fugu*. Fortunately the dish is prepared very carefully by certified *fugu* cooks, and fatalities are rare.

□ The sharp-nosed puffers of the Canthigasteridae family are common in the tropical West Atlantic, and may be distinguished by their long, pointed snouts. They are dainty little fishes, rarely exceeding 4½ inches in length. The common puffers, Tetraodontidae family, differ from the sharp-nosed puffers in having short, rounded snouts and more rounded, uniform bodies. The common puffers also grow to be considerably larger than sharp-nosed puffers. The checkered puffer shown here reaches 10 inches, and the bandtail puffer attains 1 foot. The common puffers (genus *Sphoeroides*) are most often implicated in cases of tetraodon poisoning.

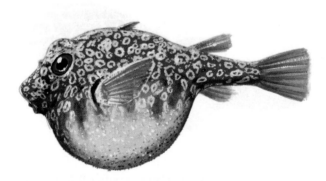

Southern puffer (tambor) *Sphoeroides nephelus* To 1 foot. Shown inflated, this is the common inshore puffer of Florida, occasionally straggling to Alabama and Mississippi shores. Matures at 5 inches. **Range:** Bahamas and Florida to Brazil, including the Gulf of Mexico. **Edibility:** poor, viscera may be poisonous.

☐ The porcupinefishes and burrfishes of the family Diodontidae are also adept at puffing themselves up when disturbed. They reach lengths of 2 feet, and it is a strange sight to see a puffed-up, spine-covered basketball with eyes and fins, paddling furiously about the reef. Of the four spiny puffer species shown, the species of *Diodon* have the longest spines, which fold back against the body when not inflated. The *Chilomycterus* species possess spines that are 3-rooted and always rigidly erect.

☐ The trunkfishes include the boxfishes and cowfishes of the family Ostraciidae. For protection against predators, these odd, fascinating little animals are enclosed in a solid, bony box with holes for the eyes, mouth, fins and vent. Their movements on the reef are curious, almost like miniature helicopters as they maneuver their rigid, boxed-in bodies with the aid of tiny, fluttering pectoral fins and tail. They are such slow swimmers that they can easily be approached and studied by divers. Some trunkfish species are known to discharge a toxin into the water when under stress. This poison, named ostracitoxin, will kill other fishes in aquaria and bait tanks, even after the trunkfish is removed. Strangely, it will even kill the trunkfish.

Sharpnose puffer *Canthigaster rostrata* To 4½ inches. Occurs in a variety of habitats, including coral reef, seagrass beds, mixed sand and rock and rocky tide pools. Prefers seagrass tips, but also eats sponges, crustaceans, mollusks and sea urchins. **Range:** both sides of the Atlantic; in the West Atlantic, from Bermuda, the Bahamas and Florida throughout the Caribbean, including the Gulf of Mexico. **Edibility:** poor.

Caribbean puffer (tambor) *Sphoeroides greeleyi* To 6 inches. This puffer is often found in shallow turbid water habitats over mud bottoms, and occasionally on shallow sand bottoms. **Range:** Greater and Lesser Antilles to Brazil. **Edibility:** poor, viscera may be poisonous.

Spiny puffer, barred spiny puffer, balloonfish *Diodon holocanthus* To 20 inches. This puffer may be distinguished from the very similar porcupinefish by the large black blotches on its back. The illustration shows a typical spiny puffer in a relaxed cruising mode, with his spines tucked away. **Range:** circumtropical; in the West Atlantic, from the Bahamas and Florida to Brazil, including the Gulf of Mexico. **Edibility:** poor, viscera may be poisonous.

Porcupinefish, spotted spiny puffer *Diodon hystrix* To 3 feet. Here is a spiny puffer in the inflated mode. May be distinguished from the barred spiny puffer (above) by the numerous small spots on its body, with no blotches. Bohlke and Chaplin report spearing a large female porcupinefish in the Bahamas which was swimming with a smaller male fish. The male companion refused to leave his mate, and swam around close by while she was on the spear. **Range:** circumtropical; in the West Atlantic, from New England to southeastern Brazil, including the Gulf of Mexico. **Edibility:** poor, viscera may be poisonous.

Striped burrfish *Chilomycterus schoepfi* To 10 inches. Very common along Carolina and Florida coasts. This puffer has been seen to aid its forward movement by expelling jets of water through its gill openings:"jet propulsion." **Range:** New England, the Bahamas and Florida to the hump of Brazil, including the Gulf of Mexico. **Edibility:** poor.

Web burrfish *Chilomycterus antillarum* To 1 foot. This fish lacks the stripes of the striped burrfish, and instead has numerous lines in a network pattern on its body, along with large dark round spots, usually 3, on each side. **Range:** Bahamas and Florida to Brazil. **Edibility:** poor.

Smooth trunkfish (chapin) *Lactophrys triqueter* To 1 foot. The smallest of West Atlantic trunkfishes. Has been seen to eject a jet of water from its mouth into the sand to expose the worms, crabs and other crustaceans that are a major part of its diet. **Range:** New England, Bermuda, the Bahamas and Florida to Brazil, including the Gulf of Mexico. **Edibility:** poor.

Buffalo trunkfish (chapin) *Lactophrys trigonus* To 18 inches. Often found in sea-grass beds, and highly changeable in pattern and color. Will make grunting noises when taken from the water. **Range:** New England, Bermuda, the Bahamas and Florida to Brazil, including the Gulf of Mexico. **Edibility:** considered an excellent food fish in the West Indies, but has been implicated in ciguatera poisoning.

Spotted trunkfish (chapin) *Lactophrys bicaudalis* To 16 inches. Trunkfishes are fascinating aquarium fishes, but their ability to release toxins that kill other fishes should be noted. Bohlke and Chaplin report that Bahaman fishermen will not keep the smooth or spotted trunkfishes in their live-wells, due to the toxin. **Range:** Florida Keys and the Bahamas to Brazil, including the Gulf of Mexico. **Edibility:** poor.

Scrawled cowfish (toro) *Acanthostracion quadricornis* To 1½ feet. The commonest and most wide-ranging trunkfish in the West Atlantic, highly changeable in coloration. Often found in seagrass beds. **Range:** New England, Bermuda, the Bahamas and Florida to Brazil, including the Gulf of Mexico. **Edibility:** poor.

Honeycomb cowfish (toro) *Acanthostracion polygonius* To 1½ feet. Unaccountably, until recently, this fish and the scrawled cowfish were thought to be the same species. This is the least common of West Atlantic trunkfishes. Primarily a reef-dweller. **Range:** New Jersey, Bermuda, the Bahamas and Florida to Brazil. **Edibility:** poor.

SCORPIONFISHES

Spotted scorpionfish (rascacio) *Scorpaena plumieri* To 17 inches. A common fish found over shallow water coral reefs and rocky bottoms. When alarmed it spreads its pectoral fins and displays its brilliant black and white axillary coloration, thus warning off predators. **Range:** New England to Brazil, including the Gulf of Mexico. **Edibility:** good.

This bizarre, fascinating family of fishes has been given more names than any other fish in the world, including scorpionfish, turkeyfish, zebrafish, dragonfish, tiger and lionfish, cardinal scorpionfish, rockfish, firefish, cobrafish and probably numerous others. It is a family to which many of these names do apply, due to its fearless nature, its poisonous spines, and the odd appearance and lifestyle of its members. Most if not all scorpionfishes are poisonous, and should never be handled without a net or other protective device. Such names as "scorpion" and "cobrafish" come from the venomous potential of the dorsal, anal and ventral fin spines, which can give the careless fisherman, diver or aquarist a very painful puncture wound. In the West Indies, the two largest species (the spotted scorpionfish and the barbfish) are highly valued as food.

☐ The scorpaenid (mail-cheeked) fishes are so named because of the bony plates under their eyes, and they include several hundred species world-wide. Their lumplike or rocklike appearance and improbable appendages would seem to be the antithesis of what a streamlined

154

fish configuration should be, but the scorpionfish is well-designed for its job. It is a master at camouflage, and it waits quietly and patiently in an algae-covered crevice, frequently hanging upside down, where it looks almost exactly like part of the reef. When a small fish or crustacean comes to examine the algae-like appendages which dangle from its face, the scorpion engulfs the intruder with surprising rapidity.

☐ They make fascinating pets for aquarium owners, but let the buyer beware when buying the scorpionfish. One report tells of an aquarist who inadvertently grabbed and was punctured by a scorpionfish. He immediately felt shooting pains in his arm, and eventually fell to his knees. After a tourniquet was applied he was rushed to a nearby hospital, where injections put him on the road to a speedy recovery. The Indo-Pacific lionfishes (*Pterois*) can inject venom that is extremely painful, but usually not fatal. The Indo-Pacific stonefishes (*Synanceja*) possess a venom so powerful that an agonizing death can occur shortly after a puncture. West Atlantic scorpionfishes, fortunately, are not deadly. The wounds they inflict, while extremely painful, are not serious if carefully cleaned and treated to prevent infection.

Barbfish (sapo) *Scorpaena brasiliensis* To 14 inches. The barbfish seems to favor continental waters rather than islands, and occurs from inshore shallows to 300 foot depths. Scorpionfishes can inflict painful wounds with their poisonous spines. Great care should be exercised in handling them. **Range:** Virginia to Brazil. **Edibility:** good.

155

Plumed or grass scorpionfish *Scorpaena grandicornis* To 7 inches. Distinctive for the large cirrus or "horn" sprouting over its eye. Found over seagrass beds, grassy bays and channels. **Range:** Bermuda, Bahamas and Florida to Brazil. **Edibility:** poor.

Reef scorpionfish (sapo) *Scorpaenodes caribbaeus* To 5 inches. This is a common little scorpion over inshore reefs throughout the Caribbean, but it is such an expert at camouflage, it is rarely seen. **Range:** see above. **Edibility:** poor.

ANGLERFISHES, TOADFISHES, GURNARDS, SEA ROBINS, DRAGONETS, LIZARDFISHES

Sargassumfish *Histrio histrio* To 6 inches. Found in floating clumps of seaweed, these masters of disguise are almost invisible to all but the keenest eyes. They are so voracious and cannibalistic, they will devour their own kind in an aquarium, no matter how much food is available. **Range:** circumtropical, including the Atlantic, Pacific and Indian Oceans; in the West Atlantic, from New England to Brazil, including the Gulf of Mexico. **Edibility:** poor.

The anglerfishes of the Pediculati (or "little foot") order are similar to the scorpionfishes in lifestyle, and even more bizarre. Like the scorpionfishes, the anglerfishes spend most of their time sitting motionless on the bottom, trying to appear as rocklike and inconspicuous as possible. Most of them are formless, lump-like fishes endowed with warty, prickly skins and an expert talent for catching their food with the aid of movable fishing rods which they erect over their mouths when hungry. A curious smaller fish unwise enough to investigate this curious baited fishpole is sucked into the mouth of the anglerfish with such speed that the human eye cannot follow its movement.

157

☐ The frogfishes of the family Antennariidae are excellent anglers and very adept at camouflage. They are voracious fishes, and when angling is poor they have been known to actively stalk other fishes. They commonly swallow fishes longer than their own bodies. Of 45 species worldwide, 9 are recorded from the West Atlantic. Batfishes (family Ogcocephalidae) are batshaped anglers commonly seen sitting quietly on sandy bottoms blending nicely with their surroundings. If prodded, they lurch awkwardly for a few feet and return quickly to their motionless vigil position. They eat small mollusks and crustaceans, and their lure apparently is not often used in feeding.

☐ Lizardfishes of the family Synodontidae are voracious carnivores also fond of sitting motionless on the bottom. They may even bury themselves in the sand until only their eyes protrude. When a smaller fish draws near, they dart upward, lizard-like, to engulf their prey in a cavernous mouth lined with fine, sharp teeth.

Ocellated frogfish *Antennarius ocellatus* To 15 inches. Easily recognized by the 3 large, ocellated spots and the short "fishing pole." All frogfishes are highly voracious, and will devour anything within reach. They are not recommended for aquaria. **Range:** North Carolina, Florida and the Bahamas to Venezuela, including the Gulf of Mexico. **Edibility:** poor.

□ Toadfishes of the Batrachoididae family are slow-moving bottom dwellers equipped with large mouths lined with sharp teeth. They are shallow-water opportunists, quick to take advantage of any available habitat. They are often found clustered sociably in beer cans, sewer pipes, discarded shoes and other debris. They are pugnacious and quick to bite, especially at spawning time, from June to July.

□ The colorful sea robin (family Triglidae) "walks" across the bottom on three pairs of detached lower pectoral rays, feeding chiefly on small crustaceans and mollusks. The largest members of the sea robin family reach 3 feet in length and are considered excellent eating in some areas. The flying gurnard, sometimes confused with the sea robin, also has long, expandable pectoral fins like the sea robin. It too, "walks" across the bottom on foot-like pelvic fins, using short pectoral rays to probe the sand for food. When alarmed, it spreads its enormous and colorful pectoral fins. Gurnards are members of the family Dactylopteridae and feed mostly on crustaceans and occasionally, small fishes. Dragonets of the family Callionymidae are small, often brightly colored fishes with broad, flattened heads. The lancer dragonet is a bottom dweller usually found in coral reef or coral rubble areas.

Longlure frogfish *Antennarius multiocellatus* To 4½ inches. Similar to the ocellated frogfish, but with a longer lure and more spots, less well-defined. All frogfishes are highly changeable in color, able to match virtually any background. **Range:** Bermuda, Bahamas and Florida to Venezuela. **Edibility:** poor.

159

Splitlure frogfish *Antennarius scaber* To 4½ inches. Note the divided illicium or "fishing pole" for which this fish is named. An accomplished color-changer, it can phase from pale gray to brown to reddish to solid black. This frogfish will inflate itself, balloonlike, with water, as do the puffers, if roughly handled. **Range:** New Jersey, Bermuda and Bahamas to Brazil, including the Gulf of Mexico. **Edibility:** poor.

Lancer dragonet, coral dragonet *Callionymus bairdi* To 4½ inches. Found in seagrass beds and coral rubble areas. Also seeks protective shelter under longspine sea urchins. The male (shown) has an elevated first dorsal fin; females do not. **Range:** Bermuda, Bahamas and Florida through the Antilles, including the Gulf of Mexico. **Edibility:** poor.

Polka-dot batfish, redbellied batfish (murcielago) *Ogcocephalus radiatus* To 11 inches. An odd, sluggish animal, easily caught by hand. Found over sand bottoms, seagrass, mud and coral rubble. The belly of adults is orange-red. **Range:** Bahamas, Florida and the Gulf of Mexico. **Edibility:** poor.

Gulf toadfish *Opsanus beta* To 10 inches. Toadfishes have been found nesting in tin cans and old shoes. They will snap at anything going by their burrow. Approached by divers, they croak irritably. **Range:** Bahamas, Florida and the Gulf of Mexico. A very similar relative, the oyster toadfish, *Opsanus tau*, is found from Maine to Florida. **Edibility:** poor.

Inshore lizardfish, galliwasp (lagarto) *Synodus foetens* To 18 inches. Named for its alert, lizardlike head, this fish is a master of camouflage. It waits motionless to ambush crustaceans and small fishes. **Range:** Cape Cod to Brazil. **Edibility:** poor.

Flying gurnard *Dactylopterus volitans* To 18 inches. Not really a flyer, the gurnard is a bottom-dweller that, when threatened, will spread its enormous blue-spotted pectoral fins, making it a difficult meal to swallow. **Range:** New England, Bermuda, Bahamas and Florida to Argentina, including the Gulf of Mexico. **Edibility:** poor.

Northern sea robin *Prionotus carolinus* To 10 inches. In some ways similar to the related flying gurnard, this fish is distinctive for having its 3 lower pectoral fin rays developed into finger-like tactile organs. The sea robin creeps over the bottom on these rays, picking, probing and overturning stones in search of food. Noisy fishes, they croak like frogs, especially at spawning time. **Range:** Maryland to Florida and the Gulf of Mexico. **Edibility:** considered a delicacy in some parts of the world, but rarely eaten in our area.

TUBEMOUTHED FISHES

If you should glance back while diving and see a two-foot length of brown garden hose peering over your shoulder, don't panic. It's merely one of the curious and friendly trumpetfishes that are quite common off West Atlantic coral reefs. They are astonishing fish to see, as they stare back at you with their large, independently-movable eyes set at the front of slender, luminous, tube-like bodies. Trumpetfishes are specialists at following larger fishes (and even divers) about the reefs, using them as stalking horses to allow the trumpetfish to prey on unsuspecting smaller fishes. A curious fish is sucked up in one quick intake of the vacuum-like snout.

Lined seahorse (caballito de mar) *Hippocampus erectus* To 5½ inches. Shown in rare red coloration phase. **Range:** Nova Scotia to Argentina, including the Gulf of Mexico. **Edibility:** poor.

☐ The tubemouthed fishes (order Gasterosteiformes) consist of two sub-orders: one includes the seahorses and pipefishes; the other contains the trumpetfishes and cornetfishes. The tubelike snout is one characteristic that all tubemouthed fishes have in common. They are all masters at vacuuming up their food by rapid intakes of water. Most of them possess a partial or complete armor of bony plates, and most of them demonstrate curious spawning behavior where the female deposits her eggs in a brood pouch or patch near the tail of the male fish. The impregnated father then incubates the eggs and ejects them live into the sea some 8 to 10 days later. West Atlantic tubemouthed fishes range in size from tiny adult pipefishes of one inch to huge adult cornetfishes reaching 6 feet in length.

☐ Cornetfishes are quite similar to trumpetfishes except for the blue-spotted coloration and the long filament extending from the tail. Most pipefishes and seahorses are sargassum and seagrass dwellers that are usually so well camouflaged in their weedy environment that they are rarely seen by divers. Shown here is the lined seahorse, the common seahorse of the Atlantic coast. Its usual coloration is ashen gray with delicate black and white lines and reticulations. Occasionally lined seahorses are discovered that are brick red in color. They are very rare, and one of these is illustrated. Although quite different in appearance, seahorses and pipefishes are very closely related—so closely, in fact, that seahorses are actually pipefishes with curled-up tails and horse-like tilted heads. Recently an unusual creature, the pipehorse, was identified that is intermediate between a pipefish and a seahorse. Its head is slightly cocked from the body and it has a prehensile tail, as shown below. It is extremely rare, and has so far been collected only in Bermuda and the Bahamas.

Gulf pipefish *Syngnathus scovelli* To 18 inches. **Range:** eastern Florida through the Gulf of Mexico. **Edibility:** poor.

Trumpetfish (corneta) *Aulostomus maculatus* To 3 feet. **Range:** Bermuda, Bahamas and Florida south to the hump of Brazil, including the Gulf of Mexico. **Edibility:** poor.

Bluespotted cornetfish (corneta) *Fistularia tabacaria* To 6 feet. **Range:** both sides of the Atlantic; in the West Atlantic, from New England and Bermuda to Brazil, including the Gulf of Mexico. **Edibility:** poor.

Pipehorse *Amphelikturus dendriticus* To 3 inches. **Range:** very rare in collections, thus far known only from Bermuda and the Bahamas. **Edibility:** poor.

164

BLENNIES, GOBIES, JAWFISHES

Yellowhead jawfish *Opistognathus aurifrons* To 4 inches. A particular favorite of aquarists because of its pale, delicate coloration and its preoccupation with keeping its burrow clean and tidy. On the reef it lives in colonies at moderate depths (10 to 100 feet). When not policing and bulldozing around its burrow, its usual posture is hovering gracefully 6 to 8 inches over its burrow, tail down, revolving slowly while snapping zooplankton from the passing water mass. **Range:** Bahamas, Florida and through the West Indies. **Edibility:** poor.

Most of the sharp-eyed, active little fishes that are seen darting into crevices, hovering around holes or squatting on coral branches are blennies, gobies or jawfishes. Blennies may be recognized by their single continuous dorsal fin, while gobies have dorsals that are separated into two distinct segments. The majority of the blennies are carnivorous or omnivorous bottom dwellers, and many blennies have unusual crests, fringes or "eyebrows" decorating their heads. A wide range of diversity in anatomy and behavior exists among the fifteen or more families of blennies. The West Atlantic species shown here include the combtooth or scaleless blennies (family Blenniidae) and the scaled blennies or klipfishes (family Clinidae).

☐ Gobies (family Gobiidae) are among the smallest fishes of the sea, and West Atlantic species range from ½ to 3 inches when adult. The tiniest vertebrate animal known is a Philippine goby, *Pandaka pygmaea*, which is full grown at less than half an inch. All gobies possess a sucking disk under the forward part of the body which they use skillfully to anchor their tiny bodies to coral or rocks in the surge zone. Most gobies are not seen by divers since they are small, usually hidden and well camouflaged. The well-known neon goby, however, displays its brilliant colors around large stands of brain coral, where it sets up cleaning stations to relieve large fishes of parasites. Most gobies lay elongated eggs attached by stalks to rocks and coral, and they guard their eggs until they hatch, both parents usually sharing in the duty.

☐ Jawfishes, of the family Opistognathidae, are fascinating but secretive blenny-like fishes which live in burrows on the reef bottom. They are usually seen hovering or "tail standing" just outside their crater-like burrows. When danger threatens, they dart into their burrows, tail-first, until only the head protrudes. They make excellent aquarium pets because they are such active, industrious animals, fascinating to watch. The jawfish always seems busy with household chores—chasing intruders away from its burrow; excavating and cleaning its tunnel in the sand or crushed coral bottom; dashing about and wrestling bits of rock and shell over to the burrow; spitting sand and aggregate like a miniature bulldozer.

Spotfin jawfish (traganavi) *Opistognathus macrognathus* To 8 inches. Easily recognized by the bold ocellated spot on its dorsal fin. Reluctant to leave its burrow, this fish peers out warily from its nest, or hovers over it, fins fluttering. A colony of jawfishes is pandemonium, as each fish tries to steal stones from its neighbor's burrow, amid much mock battling and threat display (but very little real biting). **Range:** Florida and throughout the Caribbean to Venezuela. **Edibility:** poor.

166

Greenband goby *Gobiosoma multifasciatum* To 1½ inches. A brilliantly-colored shallow water goby that prefers limestone bottoms, and is often discovered in tide pools. It has been found in live sponges off Curacao and among dead coral branches and the spines of sea urchins around Puerto Rico. **Range:** Bahamas south through the Antilles. **Edibility:** poor.

Rusty goby *Quisquilius hipoliti* To 1½ inches. A common goby over rocky areas and coral reefs to a depth of 420 feet. Note the bright orange spots on all vertical fins, and the prolonged second dorsal spine. **Range:** Florida and the Bahamas south to Venezuela. **Edibility:** poor.

Neon goby *Gobiosoma oceanops* To 3½ inches. A popular aquarium fish, this goby sets up cleaning stations on the upper surface of large brain corals. Larger predatory fishes come and often wait in line for the parasite-picking services of the neon goby. Distinctive for the brilliant neon-blue lateral stripe. In some instances, pairs have spawned in home aquaria. **Range:** Florida Keys, West Indies and the southwestern Gulf of Mexico. **Edibility:** poor.

Sharknose goby *Gobiosoma evelynae* To 1½ inches. Distinctive for the shark-like mouth set well back from the snout. Occasionally seen in pairs atop large coral heads. Like the neon goby, a well-known cleaner of larger fishes. Two almost identical cleaner gobies, *G. evelynae* and *G. genie* are known from the West Indies. **Range:** *Gobiosoma evelynae:* Bahamas, Puerto Rico, through the Lesser Antilles; *Gobiosoma genie:* Bahamas and Grand Cayman Island. **Edibility:** poor.

Crested goby *Lophogobius cyprinoides* To 3 inches. The crested goby seems to prefer brackish and silty inland bays and tidal creeks, and is abundant around the mangrove swamps and bays of West Florida. In Bermuda it has been found living in brackish inland lakes. **Range:** Bermuda, Bahamas and Florida through the West Indies, including the Central American coast. **Edibility:** poor.

Redlip blenny *Ophioblennius atlanticus* To 4¾ inches. It's hard not to like this comical little blenny in the aquarium, with its grinning red lips and bright eyes that seem decorated with eyelashes. A herbivore, this fish is superabundant on West Indian reefs. **Range:** North Carolina south through the West Indies. **Edibility:** poor.

Hairy blenny (guavina) *Labrisomus nuchipinnis* To 8 inches. Distinctive for the cowlicks over each eye, and for being one of the largest of the West Atlantic blennies. Encountered in rocky areas, sand and seagrass, it is highly changeable in color, from pale to near black. **Range:** Bermuda, Bahamas and Florida south to Brazil including the Gulf of Mexico. **Edibility:** poor.

Molly miller (chivato) *Blennius cristatus* To 4½ inches. Crests, ridges and fringes on the head are helpful identification marks for many of the blennies, and the molly miller is well-endowed with a crest and cirri. A common blenny over shallow, inshore rocky areas. **Range:** Florida to Brazil, including the Gulf of Mexico. **Edibility:** poor.

168

Wrasse blenny *Hemiemblemaria simulus* To 4 inches. This amazing blenny has gone to great lengths to mimic the bluehead wrasse, ***Thalassoma bifasciatum*** (see page 89). The resemblance to the bluehead is almost perfect through 3 distinct color phases from juvenile to adult (yellow phases only, not the adult supermale bluehead). The blenny even swims with the yellow blueheads, copying their swimming motions and appearance in every respect. Since the blueheads, due to their parasite-picking activities, are virtually immune from predators, the wrasse blenny enjoys all the privileges of this immunity without having to work for them. A sharp-eyed fishwatcher will note that the wrasse blenny has a more pointed snout than the bluehead wrasse. **Range:** Florida and the Bahamas. **Edibility:** poor.

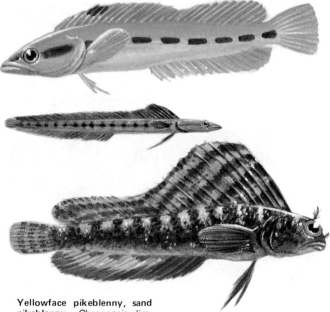

Yellowface pikeblenny, sand pikeblenny *Chaenopsis limbaughi* To 3 inches. Usually encountered in clear water areas on coral rubble bottoms or sandy areas near coral reefs. A closely related species, the bluethroat pikeblenny (*Chaenopsis ocellata*) lives in worm tubes in shallow water grass beds. **Range (both species):** Florida south through the West Indies. **Edibility:** poor.

Sailfin blenny *Emblemaria pandionis* To 2 inches. Only the male fish sports the high sail-like dorsal fin. Females and immature males are light tan with tiny, scattered light spots and dark flecks. **Range:** Florida, the Bahamas and Puerto Rico to the Central American coast. **Edibility:** poor.

NEEDLEFISHES, HALFBEAKS, FLYING FISHES

Redfin needlefish (agujon) *Strongylura notata* To 2 feet.
Range: Bermuda, Bahamas and Florida through the Antilles.
Edibility: good.

The leaping, gliding, skittering, sailing needlefishes, half-beaks and flying fishes are all members of the order Synentognathi, and they are true masters of life at the ocean's surface.

☐ If you have never stood at the rail of a fishing boat and seen a houndfish leaping after a smaller fish, then you have a treat in store. Looking very much like jet-propelled gleaming silver javelins, these 2 to 5 foot fishes can execute a series of high-speed twisting, turning, diving and re-surfacing leaps across 100 feet of water that once seen is never forgotten. They are quite possibly the fastest fishes in and out of the water. Like living arrows, leaping houndfishes sometimes impale boaters with their beaks.

☐ The needlefishes (family Belonidae) of which the houndfish is the largest member, are voracious predators and use their tremendous agility and swept wing speed either to attack smaller prey with their fearsome, slashing jaws, or to escape from larger predators. They are protectively colored for life at the surface, with green or blue backs and silvery white sides and belly. Thus their needlelike shapes are extremely difficult to discern either from the surface or from below. Their dorsal and anal fins are placed opposite each other, just in front of the V-shaped tail. If you shrink a needlefish by about 1 or 2 feet and remove the long upper jaw, you have a half-beak. Halfbeaks (family Exocoetidae) are ancestors of the flying fishes and some of them can glide 40 feet.

☐ Passengers on ocean liners never tire of watching the "bluebirds of the sea," flying fishes (family Exocoetidae), as they scull violently with their tails, taxiing to attain flight speed. They spread their pectoral fins, glide a few seconds, then splash back into the sea. At night, open illumined port holes on ships bring an occasional flying fish soaring inside. A one-pounder in flight can deal a man a knockout punch. Flight speeds of 35 miles per hour have been clocked, and flights have been timed as long as 13 seconds.

Houndfish (agujon) *Tylosurus crocodilus* To 5 feet. **Range:** both sides of Atlantic; in the Western Atlantic, from New England and Bermuda to Brazil, including the Gulf of Mexico. **Edibility:** good—in spite of the greenish-colored bones!

Timucu (agujon) *Strongylura timucu* To 2½ feet. **Range:** Florida and the Bahamas south to Brazil. The closely related Atlantic needlefish, *S. marina*, ranges from New England south through the Caribbean. **Edibility:** good.

Atlantic flying fish *Cypselurus heterurus* To 16 inches. **Range:** both sides of the Atlantic; in the West Atlantic, from the St. Lawrence to Brazil, including the Gulf of Mexico. **Edibility:** fair.

Ballyhoo *Hemiramphus brasiliensis* To 15 inches. This halfbeak ranges both sides of Atlantic; in the West Atlantic from New England to Brazil, including the Gulf of Mexico. **Edibility:** poor.

MORAYS, CONGER EELS, SNAKE EELS

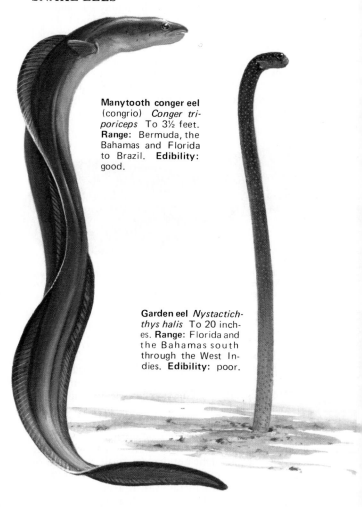

Manytooth conger eel (congrio) *Conger triporiceps* To 3½ feet. **Range:** Bermuda, the Bahamas and Florida to Brazil. **Edibility:** good.

Garden eel *Nystactichthys halis* To 20 inches. **Range:** Florida and the Bahamas south through the West Indies. **Edibility:** poor.

On a population basis, the most numerous reef animals throughout the West Atlantic are the eels of the Anguilliformes order. Due to their secretive nature, however, and their daytime concealment in reef caves and crevices, their great abundance is not evident to the casual observer. The largest and most conspicuous family of eels is the Muraenidae, or moray. The moray can and will bite with vicious, fang-like teeth. Since it almost always remains well anchored to its reef hole with its powerful tail, it is a very formidable fighter. Morays are not particularly aggressive toward larger animals, even with all their power. Most of the recorded instances where morays have attacked humans occurred when the moray was caught by a fisherman, or when a diver put a hand into its cave.

Green moray (morena verde) *Gymnothorax funebris* To 6 feet.
Range: New England, Bermuda, the Bahamas, Florida south to Brazil. **Edibility:** fair—eaten in the West Indies.

☐ Recent contacts between divers and morays indicate that these eels can be almost puppy-like. They will emerge from their caves and gently take food from a diver's bare hand. Although the moray opens and closes its mouth constantly, making it appear vicious and aggressive, these mouth movements are the moray's way of breathing by pumping water across its gills. It feeds almost exclusively on small fishes, octopus and crustaceans. The moray has an acute sense of smell, and will forage across the reef at night hunting for small, wounded or sleeping fish. A current theory holds that certain wrasses and parrotfishes wrap themselves in a mucous cocoon before sleeping at night as a protection against marauding morays and other predators. It is postulated that something in the mucous cocoon hides the scent of the sleeping fish from the hungry moray. Morays are eaten in the West Indies and many other parts of the world, but several species have proved to be poisonous, with fatalities resulting in about 10 percent of the cases recorded (see page 39, ciguatera poisoning).

☐ Conger eels of the Congridae family are easily distinguished from morays by their usually prominent pectoral fins (morays do not have pectoral fins). When the conger eel moves, it is truly poetry in motion as undulating ripples flow down the fins and the body snakes gracefully through the water. Congers have strong jaws, but lack the long, canine teeth of the morays. Garden eels are a subfamily of the congers (family Heterocongrinae), famous for their burrowing habits and the "eel gardens" they produce when many have their burrows in one patch or "garden." Snake eels (family Ophichthidae) are also burrowing eels named for their long, cylindrical snake-like bodies. Although sea snakes do exist in various tropical seas, there are no sea snakes in the West Atlantic. Mistaken reports of sighting "sea snakes" in our area are probably due to seeing the fairly common snake eel. These eels do not live in permanent burrows as do the garden eels, but they burrow easily through bottom sand and gravel, forward or backward. Some species may be seen moving freely about the reef and shore by day, notably the brilliant gold-spotted snake eel, one of the most attractive eels of the tropical West Atlantic. Their eyesight is very bad (they hunt by smell), thus they are quite harmless and may easily be observed as they pick and probe their way around sand and seagrass areas.

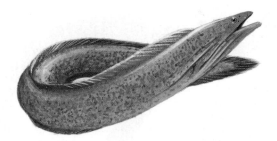

Purplemouth moray *Gymnothorax vicinus* To 4 feet. **Range:** both sides of the Atlantic; in the West Atlantic, from Bermuda, the Bahamas and Florida to Brazil. **Edibility:** fair.

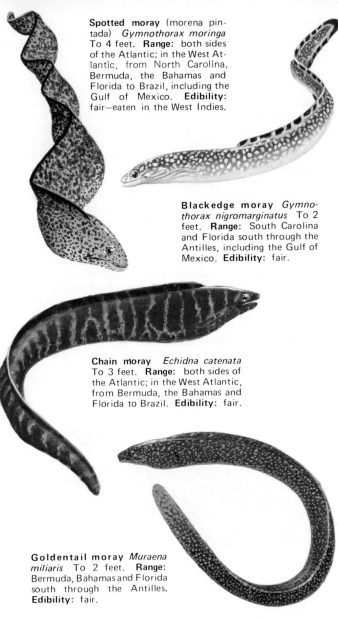

Spotted moray (morena pintada) *Gymnothorax moringa* To 4 feet. **Range:** both sides of the Atlantic; in the West Atlantic, from North Carolina, Bermuda, the Bahamas and Florida to Brazil, including the Gulf of Mexico. **Edibility:** fair—eaten in the West Indies.

Blackedge moray *Gymnothorax nigromarginatus* To 2 feet. **Range:** South Carolina and Florida south through the Antilles, including the Gulf of Mexico. **Edibility:** fair.

Chain moray *Echidna catenata* To 3 feet. **Range:** both sides of the Atlantic; in the West Atlantic, from Bermuda, the Bahamas and Florida to Brazil. **Edibility:** fair.

Goldentail moray *Muraena miliaris* To 2 feet. **Range:** Bermuda, Bahamas and Florida south through the Antilles. **Edibility:** fair.

175

Viper moray *Enchelycore nigricans* To 3 feet. **Range:** Bermuda, Bahamas and Florida south through the Antilles. **Edibility:** fair.

Goldspotted snake eel *Myrichthys oculatus* To 3 feet. **Range:** both sides of the Atlantic; in the West Atlantic from Bermuda, the Bahamas and Florida south to Brazil. **Edibility:** poor.

Shrimp eel *Ophichthus gomesi* To 2½ feet. **Range:** South Carolina and Florida south to Brazil, including the Gulf of Mexico. **Edibility:** poor.

Sharptail eel *Myrichthys acuminatus* To 3 feet. **Range:** Bermuda, the Bahamas and Florida south through the Antilles. **Edibility:** fair.

MARLINS, SAILFISHES, SWORDFISHES AND DOLPHINS

Blue marlin, Cuban black marlin (aguja de casta, espadon) *Makaira nigricans* To 15 feet. To 2,000 pounds; average 200 - 400 pounds. **Range:** world-wide in warm and temperate seas; in the West Atlantic, from Cape Cod and New York south to Uruguay, including the Gulf of Mexico. **Edibility:** good.

White marlin (aguja blanca) *Tetrapturus albidus* To 160 pounds; average 50-60 pounds. **Range:** Nova Scotia to Brazil, including the Gulf of Mexico. **Edibility:** poor. Release when caught.

The majestic billfishes are the most sought after of all the big game fishes—the true fighting aristocrats of the sea. Perhaps no other area in the world offers such a variety of habitats, such a range of excellent billfishing as the West Atlantic. Blue water fishermen comb the Gulfstream from New York to Bermuda and Bimini, and from the famed banks of the Bahamas to the rich billfish grounds off Puerto Rico. They sit patiently in deck chairs awaiting the strike of the leaping, fighting blue marlin, the sailfish and the valiant white marlin from the coast of Maryland to the marlin fishing grounds around Jamaica, through the Antilles to Venezuela, throughout the Gulf of Mexico and down the Central and South American coast to Uruguay.

☐ The principal targets of all this activity are the representatives of two fish families: the Istiophoridae, comprising the marlins and sailfishes, and the Xiphiidae, or swordfishes. Billfishes all possess a sword or bill—a bony projection from the upper jaw—that is apparently used in subduing smaller fishes. They use the sword as a club to maim their victims as they rush through a school of mackerel or similar smaller fishes. Small squadrons of sailfishes have been seen to herd schools of smaller fishes into compact balls, then slash their way through them, killing and eating in well-coordinated teams. The West Atlantic's special attraction for big game fishermen is the abundance of the splendid blue marlin. The big blue is taken off New England, North Carolina, the Florida Keys, the Bahama Banks and the abundant billfish grounds off Puerto Rico and Jamaica. The blue marlin attains a weight of 2000 pounds, although the average taken is between 150 and 400 pounds. The largest blue marlin taken by sport fishermen was a 1,085 pound fish caught off Hawaii in 1972. It was disqualified for record because more than one angler handled the line.

☐ Atlantic white marlins are the special favorites of many blue water fishermen because of the spectacular, twisting acrobatics they perform when hooked. All marlins are impressive fighters, noteworthy for their individuality in fighting compared to other game fish. Some marlins will fight the hook to the surface, twisting and tail-walking, while others will sound deep, which means a long, tedious battle. They are sought more for their fighting spirit than for their strong and oily flesh. More and more conservation-minded fishermen are releasing billfishes and other game fishes after boating them, so that they can provide additional sport for those who come after.

☐ A much smaller billfish is the Atlantic sailfish, a strikingly beautiful animal with a huge, fan-like dorsal fin. The sailfish is such a popular gamefish off Florida's east coast that the annual Invitational Masters Angling Tournament held at Palm Beach each January results in close to 200 sailfishes being caught and released in a 5-day period. Both the white marlin and sailfish are taken along the Gulf Stream, in the Gulf of Mexico, the Bahamas, Puerto Rico, Jamaica and through the Windward and Leeward Islands to Venezuela. The broadbill swordfish rivals the shark in both size and strength. It exceeds 1000 pounds in weight and 15 feet in length, although the average caught is about 250 pounds.

☐ Dolphins or dorados of the Coryphaenidae family are beautiful, active fishes that range all warm seas. They are common in the tropical West Atlantic and are taken by offshore fishermen all year, although they are most numerous from May to December. When prevailing winds blow quantities of sargassum weed, dolphin frequently accompany it. Their favorite prey seems to be flying fishes. The terrific speed of the dolphin enables it to flush the flying fishes like quail, catching them as they fall after a fumbling start or a full flight. Because of its valor and strength as a fighting game fish, and its excellent meat, the dolphin is hunted by man the world over. It is a gorgeous fish when caught, with iridescent shades of purplish-bluish gold, sea green and emerald. When death occurs, however, it quickly becomes plain gray in color. The name "dolphin" is confusing, since it is applied to this fish and to the porpoise, which is an aquatic mammal. The two totally different animals can be separated by remembering that the dorado dolphin is a water-breathing fish, while the porpoise dolphin is an air-breathing cetacean closely related to the whales.

179

Sailfish (pez vela, aguja de abanico) *Istiophorus platypterus* To 10 feet. To 141 pounds; average 30-50 pounds. **Range:** worldwide; in the West Atlantic, from Rhode Island to Brazil, including the Gulf of Mexico. **Edibility:** poor. Release when caught.

Longbill spearfish (aguja) *Tetrapturus pfluegeri.* To 50 pounds; average 15 to 30 pounds. **Range:** New Jersey to Venezuela, including the Gulf of Mexico. **Edibility:** poor. Release when caught.

Swordfish (espadon, pez espada) *Xiphias gladius* To 15 feet. To 1182 pounds; average 250 pounds. **Range:** world-wide; in the West Atlantic, from Nova Scotia to Brazil. **Edibility:** excellent.

Dolphin, dorado *Coryphaena hippurus* To 5 feet. To 75 pounds; average 4 to 25 pounds. A closely related fish, the pompano dolphin (*Coryphaena equisetis*) is almost identical to the dolphin, except it has a deeper body, longer ventral fins, and reaches only about 30 inches in length. **Range (both species):** world-wide in warm seas; in the West Atlantic, from Nova Scotia and Bermuda to Brazil, including the Gulf of Mexico. **Edibility:** good.

SHARKS AND RAYS

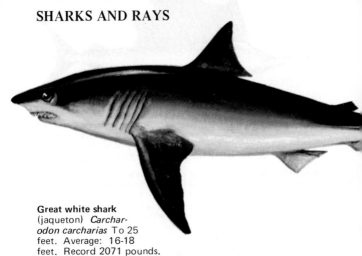

Great white shark
(jaqueton) *Carcharodon carcharias* To 25
feet. Average: 16-18
feet. Record 2071 pounds.
Range: world-wide in warm and temperate seas; in the West Atlantic, from Newfoundland to Brazil. **Edibility:** good.

For the interested swimmer who considers skin or scuba diving as a sport, probably one of the greatest fears is the shark attack. Popular misconceptions engendered by movies, TV, books and newspaper stories contribute to the image of this brute of the sea as being literally waiting offshore to pounce on anyone who enters the water, especially in tropical seas. Yet actual shark sightings around shallow reefs are rare, and incidents of attacks on humans off most of the world's beaches are extremely rare. According to figures gathered by Jacques Yves Cousteau, out of countless millions of swimmers, divers, surfers and fishermen who enter the world's oceans, only about 50 shark attacks occur each year. This compares with about 125 people who are killed by lightning each year in the U.S., and 50 to 75 people who die from insect stings in the U.S. alone. Thus, fear of shark attack off most of the world's beaches is totally unwarranted.

☐ Most sharks are not reef-dwelling fishes, but they make occasional visits to the reefs to feed on resident fishes. Divers who spear or maim fish may attract sharks to their area by the low frequency vibrations and scent trails that emanate from the wounded fish. All sharks can be

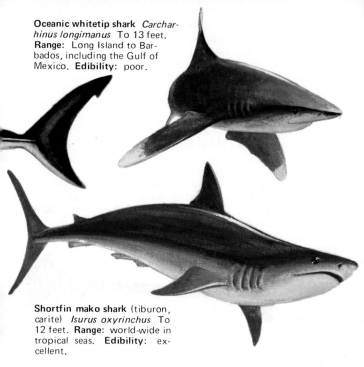

Oceanic whitetip shark *Carcharhinus longimanus* To 13 feet. **Range:** Long Island to Barbados, including the Gulf of Mexico. **Edibility:** poor.

Shortfin mako shark (tiburon, carite) *Isurus oxyrinchus* To 12 feet. **Range:** world-wide in tropical seas. **Edibility:** excellent.

dangerous, without exception, including small nurse sharks. The wise diver gives them a wide berth. Only a very uninformed diver would grab a shark by the tail, no matter how small. Occasionally divers and beachgoers are badly bitten while engaging in this risky sport.

☐ Sharks and rays of the Elasmobranchi group of fishes are distinct from all of the foregoing bony fishes because their skeletons are composed of cartilage instead of bone. Of some 250 shark species inhabiting the seas of the world, about 30 species have been recorded from the West Atlantic. The tiger shark is easily identified by the indistinct vertical bars and spots along its sides. The largest tiger shark ever taken was an 18 foot animal caught off Cuba. The great white shark is an offshore species, undoubtedly the most dangerous animal in the sea. Fortunately there are very few records of the great white shark in the West Atlantic.

□ Nurse sharks are commonly seen on West Indian reefs, often lying motionless on the bottom. Lemon sharks, reef, bull, blacktip, whitetip, silky and hammerhead sharks are some of the more common West Atlantic sharks. Like the nurse shark, both the lemon and reef sharks are capable of lying motionless on the bottom. Two roving offshore sharks are the mako and the blue sharks. The mako, a close relative of the great white shark, is a favorite of fishermen because of the spectacular leaps and tireless fight it provides when hooked as well as for its tasty flesh. The names "sand shark" and "mako" are often mistakenly given by fishermen to any of various species of sharks in the West Atlantic. *Odontaspis taurus* is the true sand shark, and it ranges from Maine to Brazil. The true mako is a fast-swimming offshore species, *Isurus oxyrinchus*, possessing a very pointed nose. It ranges worldwide in all tropical seas.

Tiger shark (alecrin, tintorera) *Galeocerdo cuvieri*
To 25 feet. Average: 10-13 feet. Record 1382 pounds. **Range:** world-wide in warm seas; in the West Atlantic, from New England to Uruguay, including the Gulf of Mexico. **Edibility:** poor.

Lemon shark *Negaprion brevirostris*
To 11 feet. **Range:** both sides of the Atlantic; in the West Atlantic, from New Jersey to Brazil, including the Gulf of Mexico. **Edibility:** good.

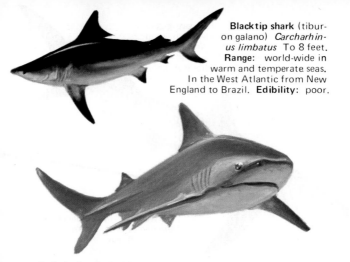

Blacktip shark (tiburon galano) *Carcharhinus limbatus* To 8 feet. **Range:** world-wide in warm and temperate seas. In the West Atlantic from New England to Brazil. **Edibility:** poor.

Bull shark *Carcharhinus leucas* To 10 feet. **Range:** worldwide in all warm seas; in the West Atlantic, from New York to Brazil, including the Gulf of Mexico. **Edibility:** poor.

Silky shark *Carcharhinus falciformis* To 10 feet. **Range:** both sides of the Atlantic; in the West Atlantic, from North Carolina to Trinidad. **Edibility:** poor.

Sand tiger shark, sand shark (dientuso) *Odontaspis taurus* To 10½ feet. **Range:** Maine to Brazil, including the Gulf of Mexico. **Edibility:** poor.

Reef shark (tiburon) *Carcharhinus springeri* To 9 feet. **Range:** Bahamas, and Florida to Yucatan and throughout the West Indies to Venezuela. **Edibility:** poor.

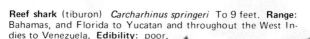

Blue shark (tintorera) *Prionace glauca* To 20 feet. **Range:** worldwide in warm and temperate seas; in the West Atlantic, from New England to Venezuela, including the Gulf of Mexico. **Edibility:** poor.

Nurse shark (gata manchada) *Ginglymostoma cirratum* To 14 feet. **Range:** Rhode Island to Brazil, including the Gulf of Mexico. **Edibility:** poor.

Scalloped hammerhead shark (cornuda, pez martillo) *Sphyrna lewini* To 12 feet. **Range:** worldwide; in the West Atlantic; from New Jersey to southern Brazil, including the Gulf of Mexico. **Edibility:** poor.

Spotted eagle ray (obispo, chucho) *Aetobatus narinari* To 7½ feet. **Range:** circumtropical; in the West Atlantic from Virginia and Bermuda to Brazil, including the Gulf of Mexico. **Edibility:** poor.

☐ Stingrays, eagle rays and cownose rays of the order Batoidei are common in the tropical West Atlantic. The spotted eagle ray is one of the most striking and attractive of the order. They are commonly seen singly, in pairs or in small schools, winging gracefully between coral heads or hovering lazily just beyond the breaker line. The southern stingray, yellow stingray and lesser electric ray are more often seen resting or half-submerged in reef bottom sand, where they excavate for invertebrates and occasionally take small fishes.

☐ All of our rays are quite harmless if left alone, but the stingrays and eagle rays possess venomous spines on their whiplike tails, capable of giving very painful wounds. The lesser electric ray has no spines, but it has

Cownose ray *Rhinoptera bonasus* To 7 feet. **Range:** southern New England to Brazil, including the Gulf of Mexico. **Edibility:** poor.

a potent weapon. It is reported to produce a shock strong enough to knock a man down, although most reports indicate much lesser effects. Manta rays or "devil" rays of the Mobulidae family are common around the outer reefs, and have often been photographed by divers. In spite of the name "devil ray," mantas are now recognized to be large, docile creatures, reaching 22 feet from wingtip to wingtip. They cruise channel areas and outer reefs feeding on small crustaceans and other planktonic food. Skates are flat-bodied elasmobranchs closely related to the rays. They, too, have widely expanded pectoral wings which extend forward to circle the head in a thin plate. The Texas skate shown is one of the more lavishly colored skates.

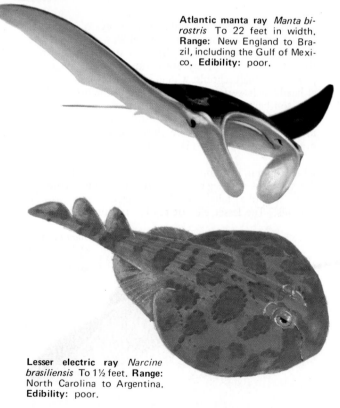

Atlantic manta ray *Manta birostris* To 22 feet in width. **Range:** New England to Brazil, including the Gulf of Mexico. **Edibility:** poor.

Lesser electric ray *Narcine brasiliensis* To 1½ feet. **Range:** North Carolina to Argentina. **Edibility:** poor.

187

Southern stingray (raya) *Dasyatis americana* To 5 feet. **Range:** New Jersey to Brazil, including the Gulf of Mexico. **Edibility:** poor.

Yellow stingray (tembladera) *Urolophus jamaicensis* To 2 feet. **Range:** North Carolina, Florida and the Bahamas to Venezuela, including the Gulf of Mexico. **Edibility:** poor.

Texas skate, roundel skate *Raja texana* To 2 feet. **Range:** Gulf of Mexico; common west of the Mississippi delta. **Edibility:** poor.

188

INVERTEBRATES

Invertebrates are distinct from other marine animals because they have no backbones. They include the corals, sea anemones, jellyfishes, clams, squids, crabs, lobsters and a host of other forms. Due to their great richness and diversity (mollusks alone number more than 40,000 species) only a few of the more familiar animals can be included here.

Atlantic oval squid (calamar) *Sepioteuthis sepioidea* To 8 inches. Often seen in small squadrons, darting like pursuit planes after schools of smaller fishes. **Range:** New England to Venezuela. **Edibility:** good.

Common Atlantic octopus (pulpo) *Octopus vulgaris* To 10 feet. A highly intelligent animal, often seen on the reef as it disappears into its burrow, or camouflaging itself expertly against rocks or coral. **Range:** Connecticut to the Caribbean. **Edibility:** good.

Scarlet lady, red-backed cleaner shrimp *Hippolysmata grabhami.* To 3 inches. A very colorful cleaner shrimp which often finds its way into marine aquariums up and down the Atlantic Coast. **Range:** southeastern United States to Brazil. **Edibility:** poor.

Banded coral shrimp, barber shrimp *Stenopus hispidus* To 3 inches. An industrious cleaner, this little "barber" is often seen picking and eating parasites from moray eels. **Range:** all tropical seas. **Edibility:** poor.

Spiny lobster (langosta) *Panulirus argus* To 21 inches. As it grows, the lobster molts its shell periodically in order to expand within the new shell. It is heavily fished and speared for the sweet meat in the powerful tail. **Range:** North Carolina to Brazil. **Edibility:** excellent.

Long-spined sea urchin (erizo) *Diadema antillarum* Spines to 15 inches. A bane to divers, who often pick painful spines out of hands and feet after brushing against them. **Range:** all tropical seas. **Edibility:** good. A delicacy in some areas.

190

BIBLIOGRAPHY

American Fisheries Society. 1970. *A List of Common and Scientific Names of Fishes from the U.S. and Canada.* 3rd Edition, American Fisheries Society, Wash., D.C.

Bauer, E. A. 1962. *The Salt-Water Fisherman's Bible.* Doubleday & Co., Inc., Garden City, N.Y.

Becker, A. C., Jr. 1970. *Gulf Coast Fishing.* A. S. Barnes and Co., Inc., Cranbury, N. J.

Beebe, W. and J. Tee-van. 1933. *Field Book of the Shore Fishes of Bermuda and the West Indies.* Dover Publications, Inc., New York.

Bohlke, J. E. and C.C.G. Chaplin. 1968. *Fishes of the Bahamas and Adjacent Tropical Waters.* Livingston Publishing Co., Wynnewood, Pa.

Breder, C. M., Jr. 1948. *Field Book of Marine Fishes of the Atlantic Coast from Labrador to Texas.* G. P. Putnam's Sons, New York.

Cervigon, F. M. 1966. *Los Peces Marinos de Venezuela.* (2 Tomos) Fundacion La Salle de Ciencias Naturales, Caracas, Venezuela.

Chaplin, C. G. and Scott, P. 1972. *Fishwatchers Guide to West Atlantic Coral Reefs.* Livingston Publishing Co., Wynnewood, Pa.

Collette, B. B. and Earle, S. A. 1972. *Results of the Tektite Program: Ecology of Coral Reef Fishes.* Bull. No. 14 of the Museum of Nat. History, Los Angeles, Calif.

Dahlberg, M. D. 1975. *Guide to Coastal Fishes of Georgia and Nearby States*, University of Georgia Press, Athens, Georgia.

Emery, A. R. and Burgess, W. E. 1974. *A New Species of Damselfish (Eupomacentrus) from the Western Atlantic, with a Key to Known Species of that Area. Copeia*, No. 4, Dec. 31.

Goodson, G. 1973. *The Many Splendored Fishes of Hawaii.* Stanford University Press, Stanford, Calif.

Gordon, Bernard L. 1960. *The Marine Fishes of Rhode Island.* The Book & Tackle Shop, Watch Hill, Rhode Island.

Herald, Earl S. 1972. *Living Fishes of the World.* Doubleday & Co., Inc., Garden City, N.Y.

Herald, Earl S. Undated. *Fishes of North America.* Doubleday & Co., Inc., Garden City, N.Y.

Jordan, D. S. and B. W. Evermann. 1896. *The Fishes of North and Middle America.* Bulletin of the U.S. National Museum, No. 47.

Jordan, D. S. and B. W. Evermann. 1902. *American Food and Game Fishes.* Dover Publications, Inc., New York.

La Monte, F. 1952. *Marine Game Fishes of the World.* Double-day and Co., Garden City, N.Y.

Longley, W. H. and S. F. Hildebrand. 1940. *New Genera and Species of Fishes from Tortugas, Florida.* Carnegie Inst., Washington Publication No. 517.

McClane, A. J. 1971. *Field & Stream International Fishing Guide.* Holt, Rinehart and Winston, Inc., New York, N.Y.

McClane, A. J. 1974. *McClane's New Standard Fishing Encyclopedia.* Holt, Rinehart and Winston, N.Y.

Metzelaar, J. 1919. *Report on the Fishes Collected by Dr. J. Boeke in the Dutch West Indies 1904-1905*, with comparative notes on marine fishes of tropical West Africa. (Reprint 1967). A. Asher & Co., Amsterdam.

National Geographic Society. 1965. *Wondrous World of Fishes.* Nat. Geographic Soc., Wash. D.C.

Poey y Aloy, Felipe. 1955. *Ictiologia Cubana.* Repub. de Cuba Ministerio de Educacion, Havana, Cuba.

Randall, J. E. 1968. *Caribbean Reef Fishes.* T.F.H. Publications Inc., Neptune City, N.J.

Sanchez Roig, M. and G. de La Maza, F. 1952. *La Pesca en Cuba.* Repub. de Cuba Ministerio de Agricultura. Havana, Cuba.

Smith, C. L. 1971. *A Revision of the American Groupers: Epinephelus and Allied Genera.* Bull. of Amer. Mus. of Nat. History. Vol. 146: Article 2, New York.

Starck, W. A. and Chesher, R. H., 1968. *Undersea Biology*, Vol. 1, No. 1, Marine Research Foundation, Miami, Florida.

Walls, J. G. 1975. *Fishes of the Northern Gulf of Mexico.* T.F.H. Publications Inc., Neptune City, N. J.

METRIC-MEASURE CONVERSION TABLES

To aid readers in converting inches, feet, and pounds to metric equivalents, the following tables are provided.

Inches to Centimeters		Feet to Meters	
1	2.54	1	.30
2	5.08	2	.61
3	7.62	3	.91
4	10.16	4	1.22
5	12.70	5	1.52
6	15.24	6	1.83
7	17.78	7	2.13
8	20.32	8	2.44
9	22.86	9	2.74
10	25.40	10	3.05
11	27.94	20	6.10
12	30.48	50	15.24

Pounds to Kilograms	
1	0.45
2	0.91
3	1.36
4	1.81
5	2.27
6	2.72
7	3.18
8	3.63
9	4.08
10	4.54
20	9.07
50	22.68

INDEX TO FISHES

194

DIVING TIPS
AND MAPS OF THE WEST ATLANTIC

The West Atlantic is a fish-watcher's paradise for the interested swimmer-tourist. Whether you are at Boston Harbor, Chesapeake Bay, the Florida Keys, the Bahamas, Puerto Rico, the Virgin Islands, Cozumel, Cancún, or British Honduras, the underwater world of the reefs is only minutes away. All that is needed is the ability to swim, and the effort required to adjust to swimming with a face mask and snorkel tube. These can be purchased at most sporting goods stores for under $20.00. Swim fins are advised for long skin-diving excursions. The fins give you the added push necessary for effortless cruising around the reefs. The warmth of the water in tropical seas (70° to 85°F) allows for comfortable swimming in your bathing suit. No wet suit is needed for short tours in the water.

To aid the fishwatcher in locating the range of specific fishes, and to select a vacation spot best suited for fishing or diving, I have provided maps on the following four pages that show the wide range of choices available in the West Atlantic. Without doubt, the best area for the diver is the warm, gin-clear waters of Florida, Bermuda and the West Indies, extending from the Bahamas through the Greater and Lesser Antilles to Venezuela. To cruise slowly over a coral reef in 80° water with 100 to 200 foot visibility is an unforgettable experience. Thousands of reef animals swarm through forests of elkhorn, staghorn and brain coral, and half an hour of slow and watchful cruising will reveal many of the fishes shown in this book.

Highly recommended for beginning and experienced aquanauts are the John Pennekamp Coral Reef State Park, covering 75 square miles of superb tropical reefs off Key Largo in Florida, and the Buck Island Underwater Trail and Park, just off St. Croix in the U.S. Virgin Islands. Both offer breathtaking underwater vistas. Further, many fish species usually associated with Caribbean coral reefs are swept up the U.S. coast by the warm Gulf Stream. Thus divers from Cape Cod to the Carolinas may encounter butterflyfishes, angelfishes, damselfishes, grunts, snappers, basses and many other tropical species, especially in the late summer and fall (August through October).

A few words of caution are called for, however, before you plunge into the surf. Skindiving is easy and pleasurable when practiced in calm, clear-water bays and beaches. Exercise normal caution when swimming near rock and coral reefs. If you aren't careful, wave action can pitch you unexpectedly into reef heads that may inflict painful scratches and wounds that are difficult to heal. Watch where you are in relation to the shore and nearby reefs at all times, and make allowances for wave action. Avoid over-tiring yourself, and always swim accompanied by a capable companion. Keep hands and feet out of reef holes and crevices, and avoid areas of high surf, turbulence and choppy water. SCUBA (self-contained underwater breathing apparatus) diving will provide even greater and deeper access to the underwater world, but the beginner requires detailed instruction and certification by a skilled diver before crossing this frontier. Qualified SCUBA instructors abound up and down the Atlantic Coast. Consult the phone book or your hotel registrar for information.